# INSPIRING//CREATIVE.WEBDESIGN 72DPI
## PAST.PRESENTFUTUREBYCHRIS.BROCK CONNECTING

**AVA Publishing SA**
**Switzerland**

**Sterling Publishing Co., Inc.**
**New York**

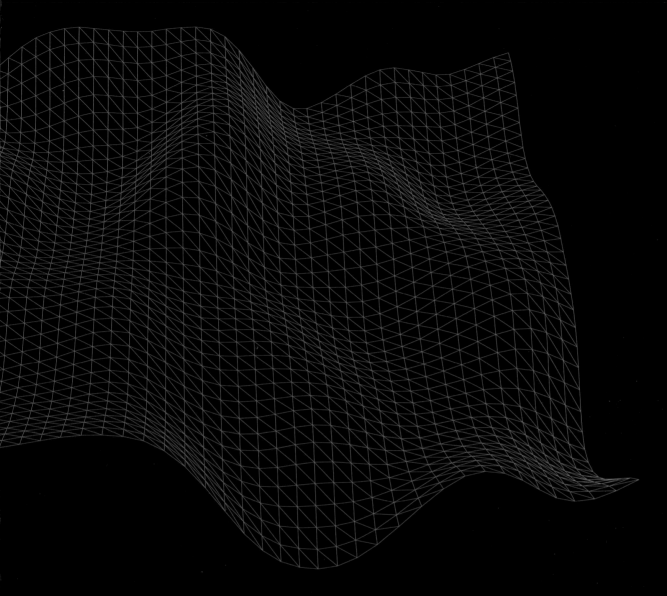

# INSPIRING//CREATIVE.WEBDESIGN <sup>72DPI</sup>

**PAST.PRESENTFUTUREBYCHRIS.BROCK** CONNECTING

[003 KB OF 144 KB, 23KB/SEC]

**Published by AVA Publishing SA**
rue du Bugnon 7
CH-1299 Crans-près-Céligny
Switzerland

Tel: +41 786 005 109
Email: enquiries@avabooks.ch

**Distributed by Thames and Hudson**
**(ex-North America)**
181a High Holborn
London WC1V 7QX
United Kingdom

Tel: +44 20 7845 5000
Fax: +44 20 7845 5050
Email: sales@thameshudson.co.uk
www.thamesandhudson.com

**Distributed by Sterling Publishing Co., Inc.**
in USA
387 Park Avenue South
New York, NY 10016-8810

Tel: +1 212 532 7160
Fax: +1 212 213 2495
www.sterlingpub.com

in Canada
Sterling Publishing
c/o Canadian Manda Group
One Atlantic Avenue, Suite 105
Toronto, Ontario M6K 3E7

**English Language Support Office**
AVA Publishing (UK) Ltd.
Tel: +44 1903 204 455
Email: enquiries@avabooks.co.uk

ISBN 2-88479-017-9

10 9 8 7 6 5 4 3 2 1

Design by Deep Creative Ltd.
www.deep.co.uk

**Production and separations by**
AVA Book Production Pte. Ltd., Singapore
Tel: +65 6334 8173
Fax: +65 6334 0752
Email: production@avabooks.com.sg

## ACKNOWLEDGEMENTS

This book is dedicated to Claire Sutton, and to the family and memory of Shea Lewis, who is dearly missed.

Thanks to Natalia Price-Cabrera at AVA Publishing for guidance throughout the project, without whom I wouldn't have known where to begin. Thanks too to Brian Morris, Publisher at AVA Publishing for supporting this project. Special thanks to Grant Bowden at Deep Creative Limited who has transformed this book into a thing of beauty.

Also, many thanks to all those who contributed, provided images and answered long and boring questions about the Web and their work, particularly Danny Brown, Mike Cina, Andrew Johnstone, Matt Owens, Damian Stephens, Andy Polaine and Ant Rogers. Thanks to Lars van Hoidonk for keeping things moving while I was away.

Finally, special thanks go to Neil Gillespie, Scott Morris, Alex Tanner, Susannah Hart and Angela Gilling from New Media Creative magazine, who inspired me to get involved in this field in the first place.

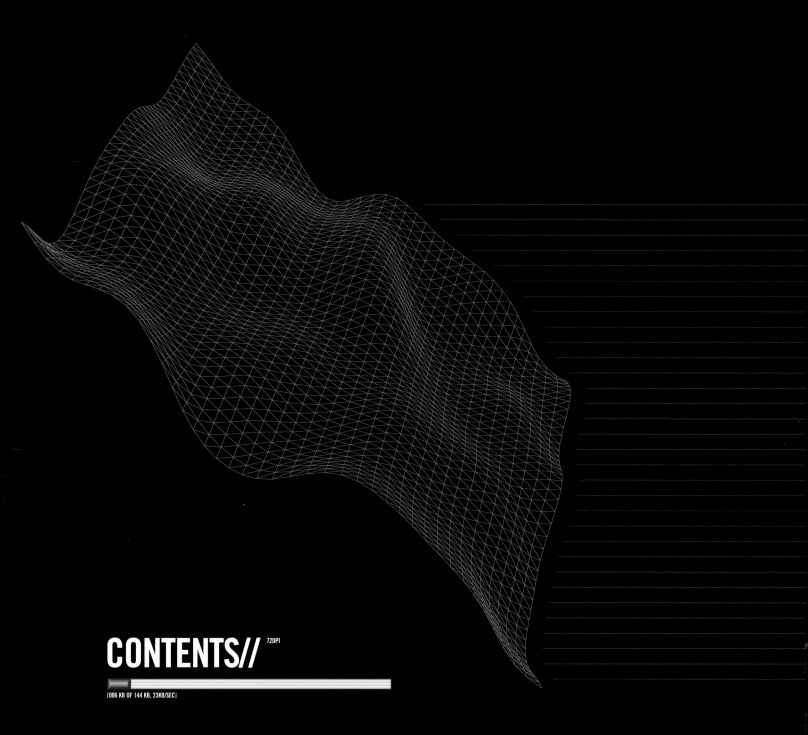

# CONTENTS// <sup>72DPI</sup>

[006 KB OF 144 KB, 23KB/SEC]

# FOREWORD

Design has always been the realm of the select few. To be a designer, you had to know the principles, the practitioners and the movements. You needed relevant accreditation from a relevant school or college, and you needed access to the tools and conduits of creation and distribution, expression and recognition.

When Gutenberg developed moveable type in 1452, he ushered in a brave new world of design. At first it was grey with simple black type, but now it's an all singing all dancing, multi-coloured, flashing interactive global phenomenon; the Web has come of age. Structure, logic and creativity collide in a kaleidoscope of possibility.

But as the Web has entered our lives, designers have split in two. There are those who have refused to extend their skill-sets to accommodate this new medium, this new angle of design, refusing to incorporate the viewer's actions into what they do. These traditionalists don't see designing for the Web as real design, but rather a pseudo, aspirational subset of those who wish to become designers and become regarded as designers, but lack the relevant knowledge of principles, practitioners and movements, and lack the accreditation, the tools and the talent.

To the paper-based designer the Web is the undiscovered country. But some choose to embrace it, and those that do find that its creative boundaries are determined only by how far they wish to go. Yes, it's true that five years from now today's sites may appear antiquated and unsophisticated, but good design will always remain good design.

Those designers who have embraced interactive Web design are joining myriad other designers like them who wish to make the most of this comparatively new, blank canvass, without wanting to wait for it to become an old, traditional medium before they get involved.

But these Web designers aren't the only people taking their talent online. Indeed there are thousands of talented but untrained individuals calling themselves Web designers, and there are thousands of creatives publishing their work online, and there are thousands of people who are finding this technology a perfect place to express themselves. And there are millions of people sitting back and watching as this creative world evolves and grows. And as the Internet becomes increasingly accessible by the day, there is a literal community of individuals and collectives publishing their creative efforts for the benefit of the rest of the globe.

But as there was a split amongst traditional designers, and those traditional designers who decided to involve themselves in the Web, so too there are splits amongst this massive online community. Those designers who came to the Web with the knowledge, the training and the talent, can on occasion, take offence to those who are doing it simply to express and enjoy themselves. Those who do this for a living can, at times, have difficulty coming to grips with those who do it for fun.

And these fluctuations of community bonding and community fracturing follow waves of new creativity, where all come together to applaud or criticise or simply discuss what has arisen. And attitudes from the real world, affected by the economy and job markets, world affairs and current events, are often reflected in the atmosphere of this collection of creatives. In this way the online design community reinforces its truth and strengthens its viability as a microcosm of the real world.

Design is all around us. Everything we come into contact with in the real world has been designed. From the pencil we write with to the paper cup we drink from, even the sign that tells us "no entry". And through the Web a new appreciation for what is fast becoming an artistic renaissance is being born, and is growing minute by minute. Design cannot be ignored, and should be enjoyed and experienced as the necessity for contemporary life it has now become.

**JAMES THOMPSON**
Wirescape.co.uk

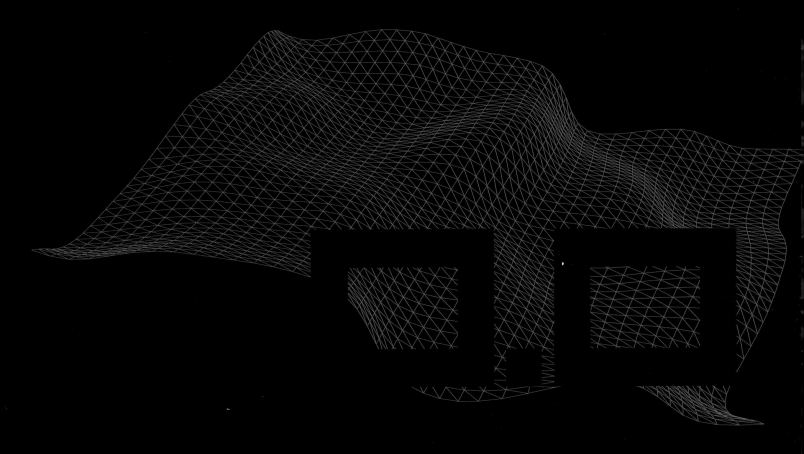

# INTRODUCTION// <sup>72DPI</sup>

[010 KB OF 144 KB, 23KB/SEC]

# INTRODUCTION

"Life doesn't simply happen to us, we produce it," says Bruce Mau of the now famous Bruce Mau Design studio, in his book Life Style. This idea has always been a motivation for designers. Through their work they have had an opportunity to represent life, to reflect, manipulate and to a certain extent control, guide and create life. In our surroundings we see examples of this, in our daily routines, the food we eat, the images we see on the television and even the chairs we sit on while we see them.

For the designer, a blank page, a lump of clay or a plot of land has always been a starting point from where one aspect of life can be grown. Whether this be in some form of art, a new house or office block, a printed magazine or advertising campaign, or even a new piece of desk furniture.

But for every designer there are always two requirements, and to some degree these have, in the past, held back some of the most talented individuals ever to have attempted to break into this arena. The need for materials and, perhaps most importantly, an audience. The designer of a chair needs pens and paper to visualise his sketches, the tools and resources to create it, and then his or her creation must be seen and sat upon. Both of these requirements need, at some level, money and support.

This had been a problem since the industrial revolution heralded the start of the modern economy, and the start of a new set of values other than simple craftsmanship and the individual's passion for their craft. Now the individual needed capital, backing, distribution, marketing – essentially, money.

**FOR THE DESIGNER, A BLANK PAGE, A LUMP OF CLAY OR A PLOT OF LAND HAS ALWAYS BEEN A STARTING POINT FROM WHERE ONE ASPECT OF LIFE CAN BE GROWN.**

When Charles Babbage unveiled the first experimental prototype of his "difference engine" in 1822, a steam powered machine created to calculate mathematical tables, he couldn't have known that he had set in motion wheels whose revolutions would change the world forever, bringing the possibility of creating quality art and design to everybody, no matter how modest or poorly funded. From this machine came the inspiration for the computers that we all use in some way today. These computers which have now become the (relatively) affordable materials for those wishing to create.

And with the arrival of computers came a distribution network so vast that its fingers reach to all corners of the globe. No continent or nation of society is untouched by the network that many of us have come to rely on. Indeed the Internet is now such a fundamental part of modern life, that we often lose contact with friends who do not have email, we miss out on the current affairs that aren't published on our favourite news website, and we become victims of information overload, from simply having access to too much data.

But the Internet, for all its flaws has provided designers and artists, good and bad with an audience. Today it seems that everybody has their own website, and with literally billions of pages of information out there, it can be all too easy to get lost in the quagmire of the true and the lies, the bland and the interesting, and the aesthetic and the gripping.

Designers have made the Web their own, bringing forth to the world a collection of the most stunning and visually exciting creative work we have known, in a form of contemporary renaissance that combines the commercial with the creative. This reflection of our modern life, where our values have become brand values, is encapsulated by the quality of work that is starting to spread across the World Wide Web, generated by design agencies and individuals alike, often with such calibre that paid-for and not-for-profit work become indistinguishable.

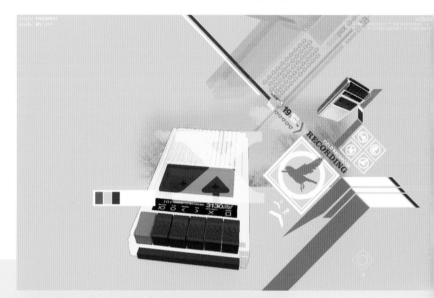

The aim of this book is to provide the reader, looking to take their first step into this world of visual stimulation that is so rich in experience, with a context to begin with. So vast is the world that it starts to describe, that to describe it in its entirety would take a lifetime of reading. Instead here is a building block, from where one may start to formulate their own understanding of this cornucopia of creative experimentation.

This book will skip quickly through the history of the Web, pausing from time to time to look more closely at some of the key creatives at work in the field. It will provide a glimpse of the tools that they use, the world that they share with their like-minded peers and the future that they are collectively working towards. From this point, a reader with little knowledge of this area may be able to walk with a little more confidence into this fascinating arena, choosing whether to get involved themselves, or to simply view the wonderful plethora of works that these artists and designers, both amateur and professional, are creating with a passion.

Inspiring Creative Web Design: Past, Present, Future hopes to provide that first sip from the cup that is the World Wide Web at its most creative, and aims to motivate the reader into finding out even more than can be covered within these pages. With that in mind, sit back, dip in and enjoy your first taste of the creative Web.

The site developed by London's Good Technology for the launch of the Sony PlayStation 2 game, Wipeout Fusion, is a prime example of how corporate clients are adopting experimental design and technologies to draw in online audiences.

However, it is sites such as Volumeone.com where the real experimentation is taking place, and the boundaries of online creativity are being pushed further and further.

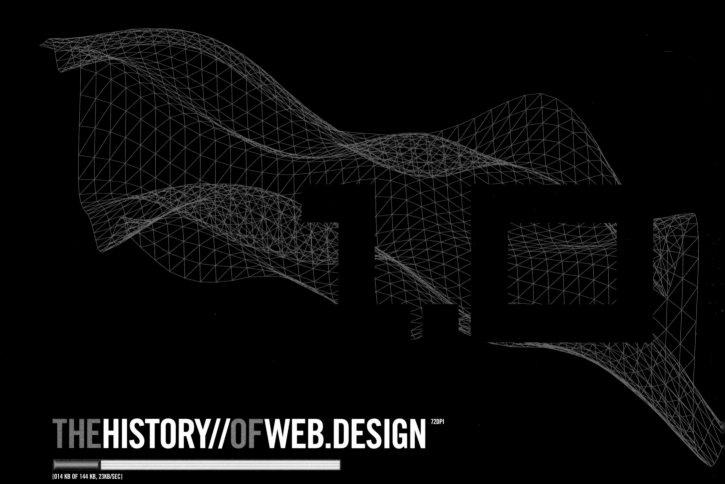

# THE**HISTORY//**OF**WEB.DESIGN** <sup>72DPI</sup>

[014 KB OF 144 KB, 23KB/SEC]

# HISTORY TIMELINE

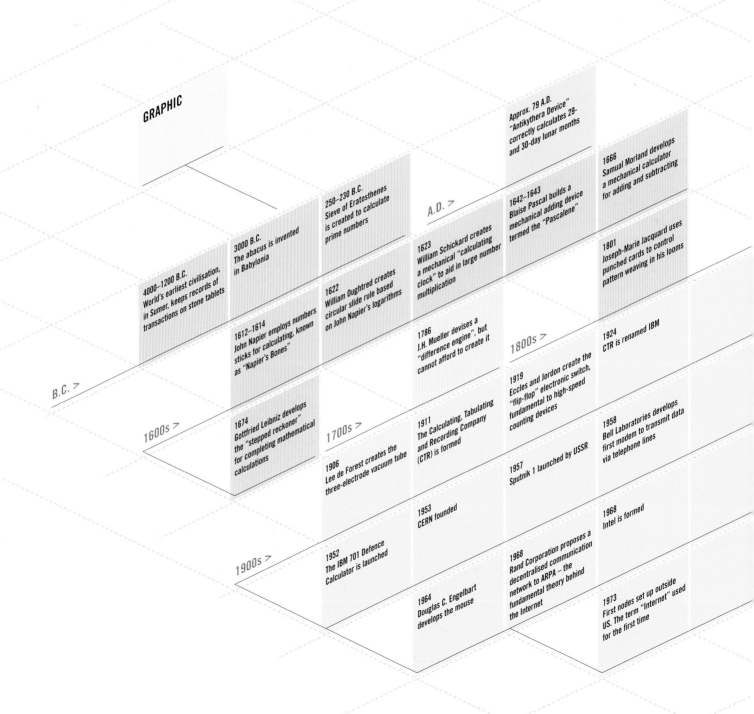

GRAPHIC

**4000–1200 B.C.**
World's earliest civilisation, in Sumer, keeps records of transactions on stone tablets

**3000 B.C.**
The abacus is invented in Babylonia

**250–230 B.C.**
Sieve of Eratosthenes is created to calculate prime numbers

**Approx. 79 A.D.**
"Antikythera Device" correctly calculates 29- and 30-day lunar months

**1666**
Samual Morland develops a mechanical calculator for adding and subtracting

A.D. >

**1612–1614**
John Napier employs numbers sticks for calculating, known as "Napier's Bones"

**1622**
William Oughtred creates circular slide rule based on John Napier's logarithms

**1623**
William Schickard creates a mechanical "calculating clock" to aid in large number multiplication

**1642–1643**
Blaise Pascal builds a mechanical adding device termed the "Pascalene"

**1801**
Joseph-Marie Jacquard uses punched cards to control pattern weaving in his looms

B.C. >

**1674**
Gottfried Leibniz develops the "stepped reckoner" for completing mathematical calculations

**1786**
J.H. Mueller devises a "difference engine", but cannot afford to create it

**1911**
The Calculating, Tabulating and Recording Company (CTR) is formed

**1919**
Eccles and Jordon create the "flip-flop" electronic switch, fundamental to high-speed counting devices

**1924**
CTR is renamed IBM

1600s >

1700s >

**1906**
Lee de Forest creates the three-electrode vacuum tube

1800s >

**1957**
Sputnik 1 launched by USSR

**1958**
Bell Laboratories develops first modem to transmit data via telephone lines

**1953**
CERN founded

**1952**
The IBM 701 Defence Calculator is launched

**1968**
Intel is formed

1900s >

**1968**
Rand Corporation proposes a decentralised communication network to ARPA – the fundamental theory behind the Internet

**1964**
Douglas C. Engelbart develops the mouse

**1973**
First nodes set up outside US. The term "Internet" used for the first time

1822
Charles Babbage invents the "difference engine"

1836
Wheatstone and Cooke develop the electric telegraph

1856–1866
First submarine transatlantic cable laid between US and UK

1947
The magnetic drum memory storage device is developed

1941
Konrad Zuse builds the Z3, the first programmable digital computer

1964
IBM launches first Computer Aided Design (CAD) system

1937
John Vincent Atanasoff devises principles for an electronic digital computer

1963
Douglas C. Englebart formulates idea about a graphical user interface

1936
Konrad Zuse devises a system of programs constructed of bit combinations that can be stored in what he terms "combination memory"

1937
George Stibitz develops a binary circuit that operates using Boolean algebra

1962
The Telstar satellite is launched, transmitting television pictures around the globe

1972
Atari, a video games company, is founded on the success of the ping-pong game, "Pong"

1960
DEC introduces the PDP-1. It is the first commercial computer with keyboard and monitor

1971
ARPANET grows to 15 nodes

1959
Xerox produces first copy machine

1971
Ray Tomlinson sends the first email

1982
The computer is named as Time Magazine's "Man of the Year"

1958
ARPA set up by US Department of Defence

1971
Intel launches the 4004 – the first microprocessor

1977
Microsoft is founded by Bill Gates and Paul Allen

1970
Floppy disk becomes available

1987
Internet has grown to approx. 28,000 nodes

1969
First communication between two ARPANET computers

1977
Apple Computer is founded by Steve Jobs and Steve Wozniak

1985
Microsoft launches Windows 1.0

1975
The laser printer is produced

1975
The Altair 8800 becomes available in kit form. This is the first PC as we know them

1984
William Gibson uses the term "cyberspace" for the first time in his book, Neuromancer

1990
ARPANET decommissioned

1973
Alan Kay develops his "office computer" that uses a mouse, a keyboard, monitor and graphics

1984
The CD-ROM is introduced

1990
The World Wide Web prototype is completed

1984
Apple launches the Macintosh computer

1990
Internet has grown to approx. 300,000 nodes

1994
Netscape Navigator, the first commercially available browser brings the World Wide Web to the world, and makes surfing the Web a reality

1983
DoD separates its own MILNET from ARPANET

1989
Andrew Milner creates Remote Access

1994
Marc Andreesen founds Netscape on the back of his Mosaic browser

1989
Tim Berners-Lee and Robert Cailliau propose the World Wide Web

1993
Intel launches the Pentium processor

1993
Marc Andreesen creates Mosaic browser

# THE INTERNET AS WE KNOW IT TODAY IS A VERY DIFFERENT ANIMAL TO THAT WHICH WAS INTENDED

## 1.1 THE EMERGENCE OF A GLOBAL NETWORK

The Internet as we know it today is a very different animal to that which was originally intended, its roots dating back further than most people realise, and certainly further than any of our lifetimes. Its story is long and convoluted, and is one of which there are many different versions, each of which has caused a relative amount of controversy and inspired many a heated debate. But to go into detail about every twist and turn of the Internet's story, recording every possible turning point, would take up a whole book in itself.

So here, then, is one brief insight into the development of what has now become an unpredicted global phenomenon that has impacted on the lives of many millions of people across the world. This whistle-stop tour will provide a basis for an understanding of our current position along the so-called "Information Superhighway", shedding light on how many of us have come to have access to what is essentially a blank canvas for a new era of interactive design.

## GLOSSARY OF TERMS

**Portal** An entry point or starting site for the World Wide Web providing links to other sites and resources all based around a certain theme or topic

**HTTP** HyperText Transfer Protocol

**FTP** File Transfer Protocol

**WWW** World Wide Web

**IP** Internet Protocol

**ANSI** American National Standards Institute

**ASCII** American Standard Code for Information Interchange

**ARPA** Advanced Research Projects Agency

**DARPA** Defence Advanced Research Projects Agency

**CERN** Conseil Europeen pour la Recherche Nucleaire

**SysOp** Systems Operator

**BBS** Bulletin Board System

**HTML** HyperText Mark-up Language

**DHTML** Dynamic HyperText Mark-up Language

**URL** Uniform Resource Locator (the Web "address")

**TCP** Transmission Control Protocol

**MILNET** Military Network

**DoD** Department of Defence

**SGML** Standard Generalised Mark-up Language

**Browser** Software for viewing websites

**CD-ROM** Compact Disk Read Only Memory

A suitable place to start this story would be 1822, when Charles Babbage instructed toolmaker and draftsman Joseph Clement to create his "difference engine". This mechanical machine of cogs and gears was built to calculate and print complex mathematical tables and is now widely recognised as the forerunner of the modern computer. Fourteen years later, in 1836, long distance communication became a reality when Charles Wheatstone and William Cooke invented the electric telegraph. The era of even longer distance communication wasn't far behind when, between 1856 and 1866, the first submarine transatlantic cables were laid between the USA and the UK.

From here, communications technology advanced slowly through the development of Morse code, the telephone, and the first satellite in 1957, Sputnik 1. Suddenly the Soviet Union had jumped the first hurdle in the battle of the superpowers, and global communication was a real part of everyday life, as satellite after satellite was launched into space to connect telephone calls around the world.

The Communist's advances into satellite communications took the USA by surprise, and forced it to create the Advance Research Projects Agency, or ARPA, as part of the Department of Defence in 1958. In these early cold-war days the USA needed to ensure its technological supremacy over the rest of the world, and so scientists were quickly put to work pushing forward scientific advances, particularly in areas such as computing and communications.

**Charles Babbage**
Charles Babbage is the father of modern computing. In the Late 1800s he developed and built a steam-driven machine of cogs and gears for calculating complex mathematical tables. From his early endeavours, others followed, leading to the development of the computer as we know it.

One such area of research was a project to build a communications network that would be able to withstand the electromagnetic pulse of nuclear strike. Such pulses were known to literally fry any electronic system with a microchip, and so a practical method of maintaining nationwide communication during times of war needed to be found. As a result a network of computers was developed that didn't rely on a central hub to control it, and across which data could travel via any number of different routes. Should one section of the network become inoperable, information could still get from A to B any number of different ways. Thus ARPANET was born with four nodes at the University of Utah, the Stanford Research Institute, University College Los Angeles and the University of California Santa Barbara. But these weren't the days of "plug-and-play" and the network, though tiny by today's standards, was still highly unstable. Charles Kline was the first person to operate ARPANET, on October 29th 1969, by entering the command LOGIN. As he got to the letter G, the whole system crashed.

Two years later ARPANET had grown to 15 nodes, another year after that it had reached 40. In 1973 two nodes, one at the Royal Radar Establishment in Norway and one at University College London illustrated the potential international reach of this new technology, and for the first time some were already referring to it as the Internet.

As the speed of the Internet's growth increased, so too did the development of technologies to run it, and on it. Reliable email software was developed, Internet Protocol (IP) and Transmission Control Protocols (TCP) for the encoding and decoding of data was produced, and suddenly it became apparent that this was no longer simply a military project. It had become a global communications tool being used by academics to share information, before the military even got their hands on it. Other networks started to connect to the Internet using the TCP/IP protocols and, since this network had no centralised control hub, there was little the military could do to regain command. By 1983, the military had given up attempting to control the Internet, and separated its own MILNET from it.

IMAGES COURTESY OF CERN, GENEVA

<u>CERN</u> (above & right)
The CERN facility near Geneva, Switzerland is the birth place of the World Wide Web as we know it today. Developed as an efficient way of managing the huge amounts of data produced by the facility's 27km long particle accelerator, it has become the face of the Internet as we all recognise it.

In 1987 the Internet had grown to around 28,000 nodes and by 1990
there were 300,000, but it was still very different from what we are used
to today. There was no graphical interface and it still needed a certain
amount of technical knowledge to operate. The user interface that we
are all accustomed to was still unheard of, and the words "World Wide
Web" had never been uttered.

Tim Berners-Lee and Robert Cailliau were working in the Electronics
and Computing for Physics (ECP) division of the European Nuclear
research facility, CERN. The scientists there were already using the
Internet to share their data, but such was the amount of information,
wading through it all had become a logistical nightmare in itself.
So they were asked to develop a system for the scientists at the particle
physics laboratory to access and share information in a much more
visual and easily understandable way. Borrowing ideas from such
influential names as Ted Nelson (creator of hypertext), Vannevar Bush
(the originator of the concept of a visual storage and retrieval network)
and Douglas C. Englebart (who dreamed about and put together a
working model of our now familiar graphical user interface as long
ago as 1963), Berners-Lee and Cailliau went to work.

PROVIDE THE BASIC
TOOLS AND LET THE
DEVELOPER BUILD
THE REST. THE TRICK
IS TO PROVIDE A
FRAMEWORK THAT
IS AS UNRESTRICTIVE
AS POSSIBLE,
YET PROVIDES A
FEATURE SET THAT
IS SELF-SUSTAINING

ANDREW MILNER

## 1.2 DIAL-UP BBS SYSTEMS

Even before Berners-Lee and Cailliau had been assigned the project, computer users around the world were desperate to connect to each other's machines, to share information on topics from science to games, their hobbies, interests and opinions. So individuals set up their own Bulletin Board Systems, or BBS, which used a standard telephone line and could be dialled into by their peers.

The software that became virtually the global standard for home BBS system operators (SysOps) was called Remote Access, and had been developed by another enthusiast, Andrew Milner. He had found that similar applications didn't suit his particular needs, and by developing this software for himself, he found that he was answering the needs of many others like him. He had created a system that was ultimately customisable by the user and had provided the bare bones for others to create their own systems upon.

"It was 1989 during my second year of university, when I finally sat down and decided to just do it," says Milner. "I'd been running a BBS for about a year using a piece of software called QuickBBS. After a while my BBS grew to a point where I needed more than one incoming line, something that QuickBBS wasn't so good at. I wasn't spending too much time at university, so at first I set out to duplicate Quick's functionality, but more importantly extend it to be multi node capable. Ultimately of course it became much more than that."

**Andrew Milner**
Andrew Milner was instrumental in the development of shared online experiences. When he created the Remote Access dial-up Bulletin Board System, he opened up a world of computers where enthusiastic individuals could share files, messages and information – all without using the Internet.

What started out as a personal project became Milner's job for more than five years, and thousands of BBS systems around the world employed his creation and soon a network of these systems had grown before the Internet ever reached the public eye. It wasn't able to handle graphics, but sysops found their own ways around that, creating a plethora of unique environments, each as individual as their maintainers. As the Web became more accessible, and attention turned away from BBS to Internet sites, Milner saw a repeat of what had happened with his Remote Access.

"I think one of the reasons those BBS systems were so popular," explains Milner, "and the reason that the Web is so popular today, at least from the developer's point of view, is that the basic philosophy hasn't really changed in 15 years. Provide the basic tools and let the developer build the rest. The trick is to provide a framework that is as unrestrictive as possible, yet provides a feature set that is self-sustaining. A simplistic analogy – most display technologies today only have three basic display elements – red, green and blue. All the manufacturer has to worry about is providing the best possible support for displaying those three colours, yet the content provider can create any picture that can be imagined from those basic building blocks."

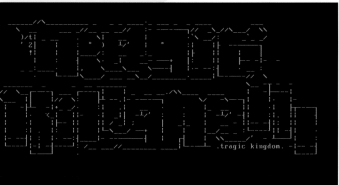

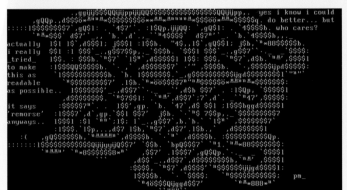

# I THINK ONE OF THE REASONS THOSE BBS SYSTEMS WERE SO POPULAR AND THE REASON THAT THE WEB IS SO POPULAR TODAY, AT LEAST FROM THE DEVELOPER'S POINT OF VIEW, IS THAT THE BASIC PHILOSOPHY HASN'T REALLY CHANGED IN 15 YEARS ANDREW MILNER

lordjazz.acid!

ld!

h   a   z   e

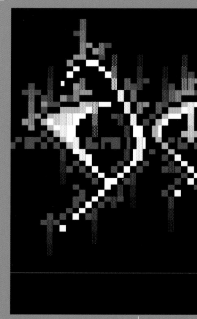

ra<acid>

generatio

elitelandia!@

artist: the silent killer

//THE WHOLE POINT OF REMOTE ACCESS WAS TO GIVE THE SYSOP
THE BASIC TOOLS AT A FAIRLY LOW LEVEL. THE RESULT WAS YOU COULD
**BUILD ALMOST ANYTHING YOU COULD IMAGINE** ANDREW MILNER

# ANSI AND ASCII ART, AND THE CREATIVE SYSOP

CASE STUDY// DESIGN.JULIAN YAP // SOFTWARE.REMOTE ACCESS BBS SOFTWARE

Dial-up BBS systems were essentially text-based, but many sysops wanted to add a more graphical element to their systems. Two standards, which are globally accepted as the means of transmitting and receiving text characters around the world came to the rescue: ASCII and ANSI. These standards meant that characters could be assigned colours, behaviours (such as flashing on and off) and identities that would be accepted by any computer anywhere in the world. Like the early video games, sysops used arrangements of these letters, numbers, character symbols and solid blocks to create chunky images. However basic this may sound, the results were, in some cases, surprisingly artistic. Some BBS hosts went to such extremes in their creative efforts, that the software they were using often became nearly unrecognisable.

As Andrew Milner, the creator of Remote Access BBS software, comments: "The whole point of Remote Access was to give the sysop the basic tools at a fairly low level. The result was you could build almost anything you could imagine – and in many cases it was simply impossible for the end user to determine what BBS software was being used because the sysop had been so creative."

## 1.3 FROM FLEET STREET TO THE SUPERHIGHWAY –
## HTML AND BEYOND

Back at CERN, Berners-Lee and Cailliau had begun creating their new visual method of representing the Internet, and there were several requirements that they had to meet. Firstly, they had to create a way in which users of the Internet could access different nodes other than using the IP (Internet Protocol) address that consisted of numbers separated by periods, such as 121.33.1944.7. So they created the Uniform Resource Locator, or URL. The URL replaced the long and easily forgettable string of numbers with a more user-friendly domain name, or the Web address we are all now accustomed to. These domain names are listed in directories at a number of certain nodes on the Internet, and when a user enters it into his or her computer, the directory is searched and the appropriate IP address found before sending the user to the correct location.

The next step for the pair from CERN was to create some way in which the plain text could be viewed in a more graphical and eye pleasing manner. So they looked to another industry that had developed a method for controlling the appearance and position of text and images, the print publication industry.

THIS EXTREMELY
SIMPLE LANGUAGE
WAS CALLED
HYPERTEXT MARK-UP
LANGUAGE, OR HTML,
AND IT BECAME
THE FUNDAMENTAL
BUILDING BLOCK
FOR ALL DESIGNERS
WHO DECIDED TO
TAKE THEIR WORK
TO THE WEB

In the print industry a standard set of rules had been developed for laying out pages of newspapers and magazines, and it was called Standard Generalised Mark-up Language, or SGML for short. Using SGML codes in the printing systems, page editors were able to accurately instruct automated printing presses how text should be displayed; whether it should be large or small, what font to use, should it be bold, italic or underlined, what colour should the background be, and where should the pictures go in relation to the page and at what size.

This language was cannibalised by Berners-Lee and Cailliau and adapted for use with hypertext. So now what it did was not only indicate where and how images and text should be displayed, but also how they should respond when clicked or rolled over with the mouse, what other pages of information should be linked to when clicked, and what other behaviours objects within a page should have. They called this extremely simple language Hypertext Mark-up Language, or HTML, and it became the fundamental building block for all designers who decided to take their work to the Web. Suddenly people who had been previously struggling to create their work with other complicated programming languages for CD-ROMs or floppy disks, or who had been fumbling around with ASCII art on their BBS, found a new, easy-to-understand and program world lay waiting for them to take advantage of.

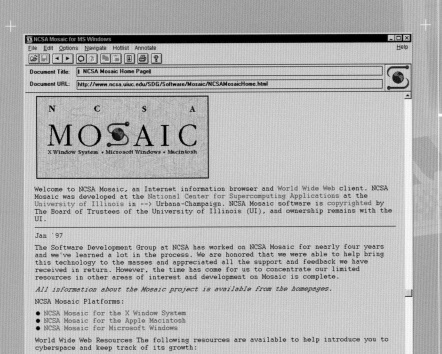

# THE FIRST BROWSERS
## CASE STUDY// DESIGN.MARC ANDREESEN

The World Wide Web, as developed by Berners-Lee and Cailliau was still a textual animal. They had created an easy method of cross-referencing and accessing information for academics, but it was not a visual medium as we know it to be today.

That was until Marc Andreesen, a 22-year-old undergraduate created the "Mosaic" browser in 1993. Mosaic was the first browser as we recognise them today, and really turned the Web into a multimedia environment. His browser could display images, and interpret HTML enough to play sounds and even basic animations.

The work he did on Mosaic can still be seen in the browsers since developed by Microsoft (undoubtedly the market leader) and Netscape, whose Navigator program was the first commercially successful browser on the market. Now Opera has joined the ranks to become the third of the most commonly accepted browsers available, free, to anyone who surfs the net.

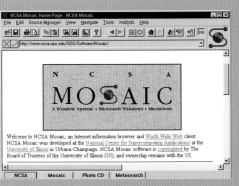

**Mosaic: 1993**
Mosaic, developed by Marc Andreesen with the National Center for Supercomputing Applications at the University of Illinois, was introduced at a time when the Web had only 200 servers. Within a year the browser had several million users and had been instrumental in creating the Internet as it is recognised today.

**Opera: 1994**
Opera was developed by Jon S. von Tetzchner and Geir Ivarsøy for private use by Norwegian telecom Telenor. It wasn't released publically on the Internet until 1996, when its claims as the world's fastest browser were put to the test by users of Microsoft Windows. Now available for most platforms, it is ranked among the most popular of all browsers.

**Microsoft Internet Explorer: 1995**
Originally developed under the code name "O'hare" (after Chicago's O'hare airport) Explorer was released as an add-on to Microsoft Windows 95 (pre-release code name, "Chicago"). While this first version was not popular with many users, who preferred to use Mosaic and Opera, Microsoft's commitment to refining its browser has seen it grow in popularity. So much so, in fact, that it is now the most popular browser on the planet, with many sites designed specifically to work with it, and nothing else.

FREEDOM OF
EXPRESSION WAS
AVAILABLE TO ANYONE
WHO WISHED TO LOOK,
AND THE ABILITY TO
INFLUENCE THE WORLD
WAS OPEN TO ALL

## 1.4 INNOVATORS AND ORIGINATORS

It wasn't long after the creation of the World Wide Web that designers found they could take their work online and bring it to life by allowing people to interact with it. Suddenly they were no longer simply designers, but had become Interaction Designers. Now they found that publishing their work to millions around the world didn't require the marketing budget of a major corporation, just a little determination and a little trial and error getting to grips with the technicality of it all. This newfound freedom of expression was available to anyone who wished to look, and the ability to influence the world was open to all.

Sites started to appear, such as the text-based Word.com, whereby designers and authors could begin to experiment with engaging narrative, catering for a new audience with new interests. Experimentation into areas such as linearity and illogical progression came from sites such as Jodi.org and the now famous etoy.com, where concept ruled over design quality, and the idea that you didn't have to be a qualified artist to get involved was starting to take seed.

**Jodi.org**
This was one of the first sites to make the most of the Web as a space for graphical creative expression. Though the site can often be confusing, disorienting and even unpleasant to experience, it is this raw edge that reflects the inner workings of the computer's own language.

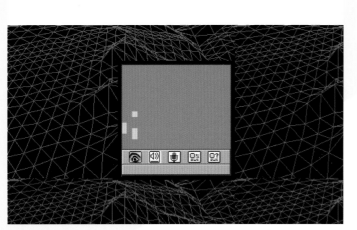

# WWW.ETOY.COM

The etoy Corporation is a strange entity. Created by seven individuals who rarely meet, the group's slogan is "incubations and surreal business activities reflecting the net and society since 1994". Despite this intriguing insight into etoy, it is hard to explain exactly what it does. Perhaps it is easier, then, to attempt to paint a picture of the group by examining what they have done.

In 1994 the etoy Corporation was created to be one of the most surreal and confusing dot.com ventures in the history of the Internet. Its aim, to establish a complex and self-generating "art virus and e-brand" that reflected the nature of modern life and business. Such was the nature of etoy, that even its name was created by a computer program that combined a vast number of short words and letters and presented possibilities that fell within flexible parameters. The founders then spent 15 hours talking in an Internet chat-room trying to decide which was the most appropriate name. Obviously "etoy" won.

The founders of etoy worked around the globe in five European cities and one American city, and through their creation attempted to merge their various roles as sound-producers, architects, artists, lawyers, and designers into one digital identity. Selling their own personal identities to their new corporation, any work that they produced was the product of etoy, and not their own.

Through this theory of bringing all these various fields of interest and work under one brand, etoy is virtually limitless in what it can set out and do. It has blurred the boundaries between business and art, individual and corporation, and was one of the first conceptual art groups to employ the Internet in such a way. Indeed, such is their belief in the net as a location-less entity, the group only met on three occasions in Bratislava, Linz/Varna and Budapest to sign the contracts tying them to the project.

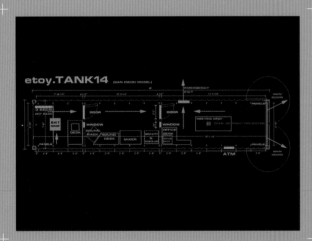

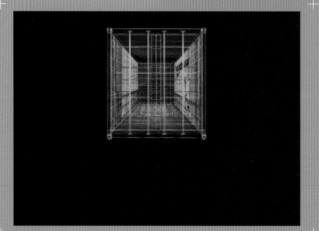

PORATION

E-UNIT, or 1/32'000'000 of the

94 - encourages the playful and
gamble with cultural assets, alter the
cial and cultural values.

**etoy.VALUE-SYSTEM**

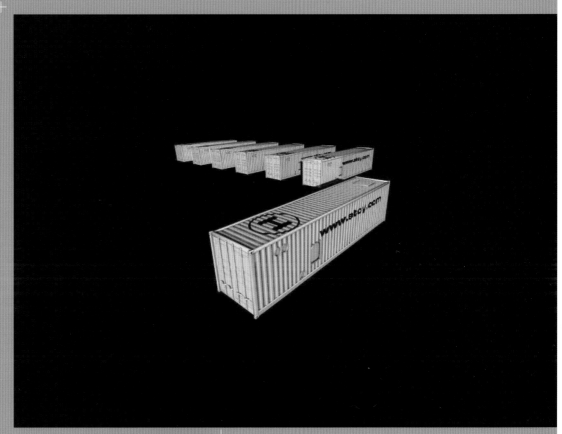

etoy.DAY-CARE

"BIG SOCIAL GAME"

Biennale Internazionale Arte Giovane
TORINO 19. APRIL - 19. MAY 2002

...the first test generation will be recruited and trained by etoy AGENTS within the next 5 days.
come back to study the pool of acquired research data.

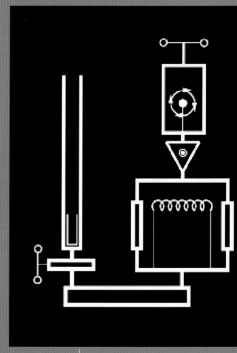

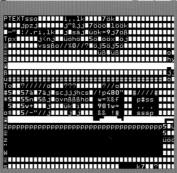

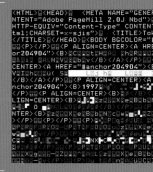

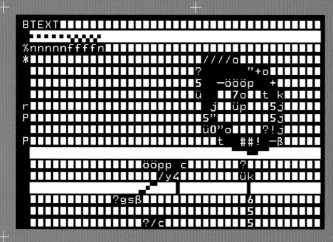

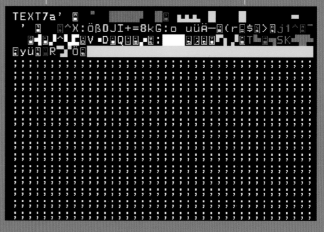

# WWW.JODI.ORG

**CASE STUDY// DESIGN.JOAN HEEMSERK & DIRK PAESMANS // SOFTWARE.HTML**

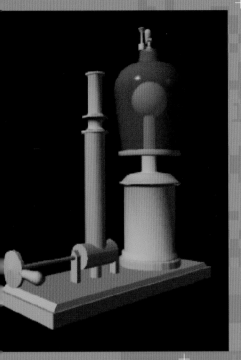

Jodi is considered by some to be the most famous art site on the net. But anyone who goes there will see little traditional artistic values in this most confused and non-aesthetic of domains. Perhaps it is better to see the art, created by Barcelona-based Joan Heemserk and Dirk Paesmans, as being in the concept. It is non-linear, and there is little narrative to be found here. Indeed, this is considered the point, as visitors stumble from page to confused page of mixed-up graphics and text.

There is little to make sense of within Jodi, but perhaps this is the reasoning behind the site's popularity. It is easy to see the connection with screen after screen of what appears to be random characters and digits, mimicking the language of the computer itself. Colours reflect the early low-colour monitors, from greens of the first terminals, to the vivid blues and yellows of the first home computers.

What Jodi does is to create a world that represents what we are really seeing whenever we stare at our VDU. A mishmash of computer code that we normally expect to see hidden behind its more accessible interpretations, and suddenly we find ourselves jarred away from the user-friendly companion that sits on our desktops. Here is a truth, maybe the truth, behind the mind of the computer in every home, school and office. As much as we think we understand the computer, we can never really think as it does.

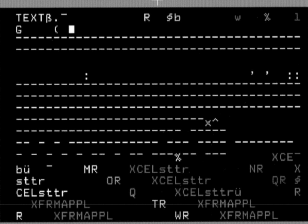

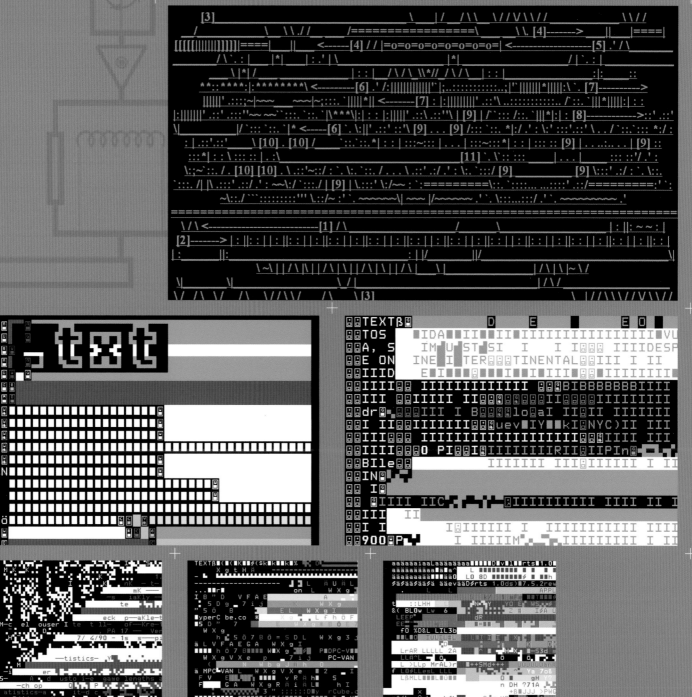

//AS MUCH AS WE THINK WE UNDERSTAND THE COMPUTER,
WE CAN NEVER REALLY THINK AS IT DOES

AntiRom, a collective from the UK which had begun making interactive CDs at London's Westminster University, wanted to explore the idea of interaction design further, and saw that there could be a commercial market for their artistic experiments. After applying for and receiving a grant from the Arts Council of Great Britain, they set about learning this new medium, and soon were taking on clients such as London's Science Museum, for whom they created touchscreen electronic kiosk installations for an exhibition titled the Challenge of Materials. The kiosks, created in 1996 and 1997, are still there today.

As sites started appearing and people began to play with what was available to them, a new "net culture" started to appear. Ideas were being shared, concepts discussed and a new set of ideas and rules about expression began to develop. To be published you didn't necessarily need critical acclaim behind you, simply motivation and a good idea.

## AS SITES STARTED APPEARING AND PEOPLE BEGAN TO PLAY WITH WHAT WAS AVAILABLE TO THEM, A NEW "NET CULTURE" STARTED TO APPEAR. IDEAS WERE BEING SHARED, CONCEPTS DISCUSSED AND A NEW SET OF IDEAS AND RULES ABOUT EXPRESSION BEGAN TO DEVELOP

**Antirom/Romandson**
Eventually the creative
minds at AntiRom
disbanded, but went
on to create such
well-regarded creative
agencies as Tomato
Interactive and
Romandson, and still
pioneer with creative use
of the Internet for both
commercial and non-
commercial purposes.

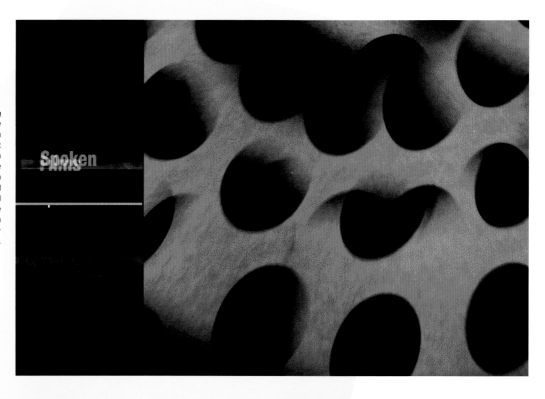

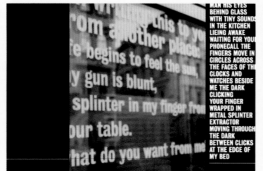

If you were to ask about tomato you might start
to think about the kind of questions that you'd
like to ask.

もしトマトのことを知りたいのなら、何を知りたいのか考
えなさい。
どういう意味、

# TOMATO
# INTERACTIVE

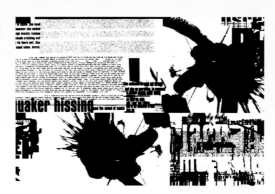

**AS FAR AS INTERACTIVE DESIGN IS CONCERNED, I WOULD HAVE TO SAY ANTIROM SET THE STANDARDS**

ANT ROGERS

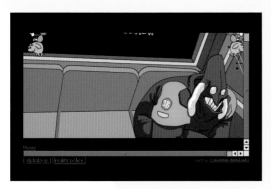

ROMANDSON

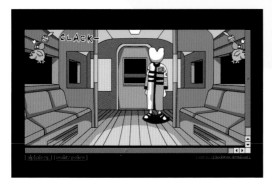

# WWW.ANTIROM.COM

CASE STUDY// DESIGN.ANTIROM // SOFTWARE.MACROMEDIA DIRECTOR

AntiRom was set up by six students, Sophie Pendrell, Tomas Roope, Joe Stephenson, Rob LeQuesne and Andy Polaine, from London's Westminster University. Together with one of their lecturers, Andy Cameron, and friends Luke Pendrell and Andy Allenson, they had been very impressed by a CD-ROM given away free with the Dutch magazine, Mediamatic. The group had already been experimenting with interactive media when they saw the disc, developed by Gerard van der Kapp, and its collection of experiments and toys, and decided that they wanted to do the same sort of thing. So they applied for a grant from the Arts Council of Great Britain.

"The grant was supposed to be for research," says Andy Polaine, now based in Australia and working for interactive agency, Thread, "but we decided to put money of our own in, press up a load of CDs and then give them away."

A couple of years later the collective, having now grown with the addition of Ant Rogers and Joel Baumann, became a company producing work that they wanted to produce, and making money from it.

"As far as interactive design is concerned, I would have to say AntiRom set the standards," says Ant Rogers. "If for nothing else, at least for taking the risk of giving it a go without worrying if it was going to work all the time."

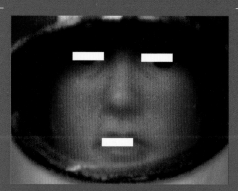

My elb
has the tensile s

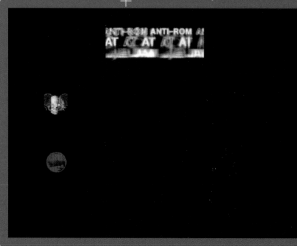

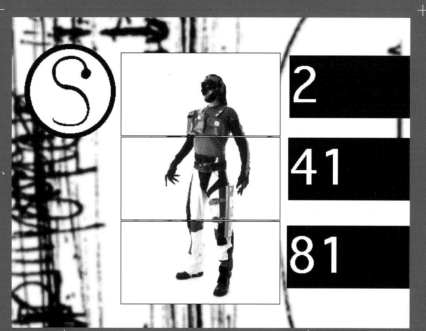

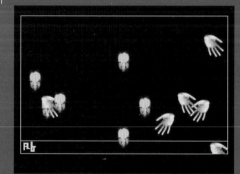
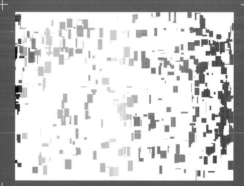
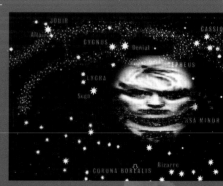

USABILITY//VS.CREATIVITY [72DPI]

[046 KB OF 144 KB, 23KB/SEC]

WHAT IS THE POINT
OF SOMETHING IF
NOBODY CAN WORK
OUT HOW TO USE IT?

## 2.1 WHAT IS USABILITY?

Usability is one of the most important issues pertaining to Web design and fundamentally it is the assessment of how "usable" a site is. Experts in the field explain it simply by arguing: What is the point of something if nobody can work out how to use it?

All the best-designed websites don't need any explanation. For the user, finding what they want is simply a matter of looking and clicking without instructions, just simple intuitive design which leads a user from where they are to what they want in the easiest manner.

But usability goes further than this. E-commerce sites have failed due to poor usability, as users have not, no matter how hard they have tried, been able to spend their money. All these elements work to reinforce an experience, whether that is bad or good, which eventually will come to represent a particular site.

**Jakob Nielsen**
Self proclaimed "usability guru", Jakob Nielsen is a founder of the Nielsen-Norman group. Not necessarily a popular man amongst designers, his claims on where sites fall down, and why pictures should be done away with online if at all possible have often courted controversy. But few would argue that when it comes to building sites that work, he is essentially right.

As Jakob Nielsen, one of the world's leading usability experts, puts it: "The thing about the Web, is that the user's action is what builds the experience."

But this does not just mean that all the hyperlinks should be easily spotted. The way that a site is organised, where a user's eye is directed on any given page, whether the user has the required plug-ins and is able to download them, and the speed with which a site loads are all important aspects of usability. The idea of fast loading speeds is particularly relevant with regards to the more creative sites, as pictures, animations and complex imagery often increase file size and therefore download times. What can result from this is a negative experience for the user who, after all, is creating their own experience from what they are given.

"The experience in interactive media is structured by the user," says Nielsen. "This is one of those tensions between the author who has their own experience and their audience. With media like books, theatre or even cinema, the experience is generally defined by the creator and presented to you, whereas interactive media is an environment which is constructed by the user's manipulation of the building blocks provided to them."

## INTERACTIVE MEDIA IS AN ENVIRONMENT CONSTRUCTED BY USER MANIPULATION OF THE BUILDING BLOCKS PROVIDED TO THEM

JAKOB NIELSEN

# WWW.DOMINICBOLTON.COM

CASE STUDY// DESIGN.DOMINIC BOLTON // SOFTWARE.MACROMEDIA FLASH

As Flash and other authoring packages become easier to use, and the idea of usability becomes more important when presenting work online, we are going to be increasingly seeing traditionally offline creatives, such as the fashion photographer Dominic Bolton taking their work and portfolios online. As with this site, simplicity is the key to ease of use and makes selling even yourself a much more successful task.

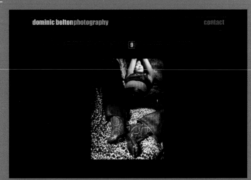

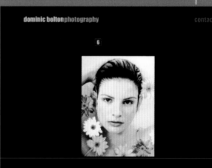

## //WE ARE GOING TO BE INCREASINGLY SEEING TRADITIONALLY OFFLINE CREATIVES TAKING THEIR WORK AND PORTFOLIOS ONLINE

VISITORS SHOULD
BE FREE TO MOVE
AROUND THE
INTERNET WITH
EASE, AS WITH ANY
OTHER PHYSICAL
SPACE SUCH AS
A SUPERMARKET
OR A THEME PARK

## 2.2 EXPERIENCE AND DESIGN

The idea that designing for the Web is essentially designing an experience is paramount. Web pages, after all, are not simply about the transfer of information from the screen to the mind of the user, and they certainly aren't about simple aesthetically pleasing images. This explains why some of the most successful sites on the Internet are also some of the ugliest, but also the easiest to use. It also explains why Experience Design has become a field of study in its own right.

If the Internet is to be interpreted as a space, or Cyberspace as William Gibson termed it in his 1984 novel, Neuromancer, then visitors should be free to move around it with ease, as with any other physical space such as a supermarket or a theme park. And as we come away from supermarkets and theme parks with an experience (whether that be good or bad) then similar rules must apply. And these rules can either add to, in good examples, or detract from, the value of the information we are being presented with.

Looking at Amazon.com, the quality of the experience keeps the user coming back each time they wish to buy a book or other product. The ease with which they can find what they want often beats even the best bookshops, and the speed with which the site delivers on its promises – something which goes beyond the screen and into the physical world of postage and packaging – leaves the user feeling good about the site they have just visited, and often they will call again. This user retention is commonly known as "stickiness". The user comes to the site, stays there, and comes again when they need to access those services a second time.

**SOME OF THE MOST SUCCESSFUL SITES ON THE INTERNET MIGHT BE SOME OF THE UGLIEST, BUT THEY ARE ALSO SOME OF THE EASIEST TO USE**

This idea of creating a positive "experience" is deemed so important in some corners of the Web design world, that the American Institute of Graphic Arts (AIGA) has even gone to the effort of turning the theory into a movement. While there is still division amongst Web creatives as to whether they are "experience designers" or "interaction designers" some fundamental issues have emerged that are agreed upon by all. Through its Experience Design Group, AIGA works with designers from all sectors – including entertainment, commerce, database development – to create answers to questions that still arise in this area. Each year the Advance for Design Summit brings together professionals from all walks of life to unify approaches to creating valid and positive experiences online.

Through the summit, and AIGA's twice-yearly online magazine, GAIN, four principles for producing acceptable work have been developed, and these generally revolve around the idea that a strong brand online, such as Amazon, tells a "story". In other words a user is engaged by a theme or narrative, and the experience becomes one that they understand, bond with and return to. Creating such a story provides focus for the creators of a site, and the knock-on effect of this is that all the separate elements work together toward a common ultimate goal.

As more and more of our lives take place online, it is inevitable that this will create online experiences. Thus it is important for designers to take this into account, from major corporate sites to personal portfolio home pages, a life online will be directed by the quality of experience that a user receives, so to optimise this is to optimise traffic to your site. For many this will result in increased revenue, and perhaps something even more valuable: Brand loyalty.

GAIN
GAIN is the twice-yearly online magazine from the American Institute of Graphic Arts (AIGA). It focuses on many aspects of interactive design, but its chief area of coverage is experience design. Not only does it provide information in terms of content, but also informs by example, showing through its presentation and layout how experience design can be put into practice to better engage readers and users, and to make information disseminated online more effective and valuable.

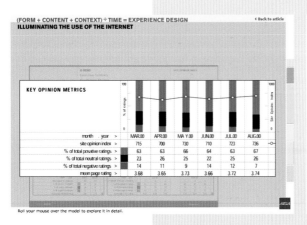

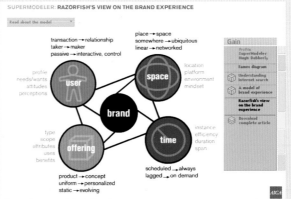

**Gain:** AIGA Journal of Design for the Network Economy

# Gain

→ Volume 1, number 1

About Gain

From AIGA
**Experience design**

Profile
**SuperModeler:
Hugh Dubberly**

Case study
**The artless
website**

Case study
**Metamorphosis**

Definitional
**Good design
in the digital age**

experience design what's that?

Join the discussion

presented by **Sapient**

## GOOD DESIGN IN THE DIGITAL AGE

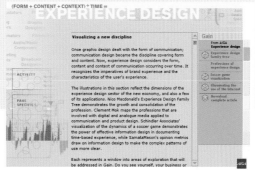

## EXPERIENCE DESIGN
(FORM + CONTENT + CONTEXT) ÷ TIME =

### Visualizing a new discipline

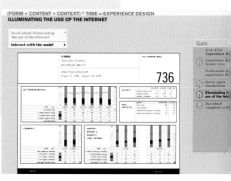

(FORM + CONTENT + CONTEXT) ÷ TIME = EXPERIENCE DESIGN
**ILLUMINATING THE USE OF THE INTERNET**

736

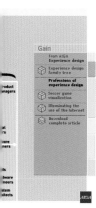

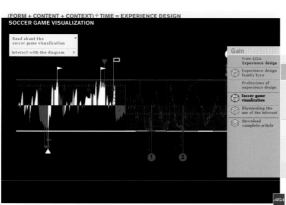

(FORM + CONTENT + CONTEXT) ÷ TIME = EXPERIENCE DESIGN
**SOCCER GAME VISUALIZATION**

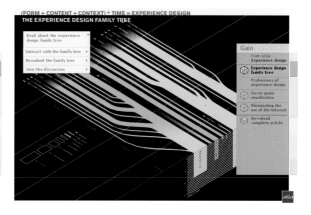

(FORM + CONTENT + CONTEXT) ÷ TIME = EXPERIENCE DESIGN
**THE EXPERIENCE DESIGN FAMILY TREE**

EMPLOYING GRAPHICS IN PLACE OF TEXT OFTEN MEANS THAT THOSE WHO CANNOT SEE, AND USE A DEVICE TO TRANSLATE TEXT INTO A FORM THAT THEY CAN UNDERSTAND ARE MISSING OUT ON PART OF THE EXPERIENCE

## 2.3 DESIGNING FOR THE DISABLED

In the real world, if a place or business wants to cater for the disabled, there are certain improvements that they can make. The installation of hearing aid loops, wider doorways, ramps and handrails all add to the usability of the particular place for the less able.

And websites are no different. Blind Web users may often use a terminal which converts text to Braille, or may require larger text sizes, or even employ text to voice synthesis devices.

Often though, Web designers overlook these needs. Many sites which display content confuse Braille terminals, which try to read the screen from side to side, unable to recognise individual columns. Text is as often as not, unscalable, and cannot be increased in size for the visually impaired. And though it may add to the aesthetics of a site, employing graphics in place of text often means that those who cannot see, and use a device to translate text into a form that they can understand are missing out on part of the experience.

While the disabled do represent a minority, they are still significant in number, and businesses that cater to the less able both online and off are tapping into a commercial market that many others miss out on. Often needlessly.

With a little thought and ingenuity, designers can create a Web which truly lives up to its reputation as being a place for all, no matter what limitations may face them in the physical world, and a place where everybody is equal. However, the trade-off may come when designers realise that the most accessible sites for the less able, are more often than not, the simpler, less elaborate sites.

Current ALA: Eric Meyer on Print Style Sheets
Current Interview: SitePoint

**16 May 2002**
[1 pm | 10 am]
Newly added to the **Exit Gallery**, two fine sites by Todd Dominey:
**Dominey Design**, a distinctive and charming professional services
site crafted in Flash; and **What Do I Know**, an elegantly designed
and intelligently written daily site built with XHTML and CSS.
We've linked to these sites **before**, but they'll be easier to find now.

Also added to the Exit Gallery: **Brainstorms & Raves**, Shirley E.
Kaiser's near-daily column about web design and development, with
a special focus on accessibility and standards; and **Scott Andrew**, a
fine daily focused on the technology formerly known as "DHTML."
Both sites should have been in the Exit Gallery for years.

Also added to the Exit Gallery: **What is a Print?** This Flash site for
the Museum of Modern Art is one of the best we've ever seen: fresh,
fun, and immensely usable. It was created by NYC's **The Chopping**

ISSN: 1534-0309
Daily Divisions:
World Tour
Interviews
Link Up
About
F.A.Q.
Mail
Exit
Bio

Jakob Nielsen Corner:
[Skin1] [Skin2] [Skin3]
[Search]

Designing With Web Standards:
XHTML/CSS Style Guide (NYPL)
Better Living Through XHTML (ALA)
Fix Your Site With the Right
DOCTYPE (ALA)

Recent Spew:
Alley of the Shadow (PDN–Pix)

The Classics:
Style vs. Design (Adobe)
If the Great Movies Had Been
Websites

Other Works:
A List Apart
Happy Cog
Independents Day
Web Standards Project

Rotating Affiliates:
5k
Digital Web
iStockphoto

Web designer Jeffrey Zeldman's site,
www.zeldman.com, is an ideal illustration
of how a site can be made accessible to those
who are less able, while still retaining strong
design values.

The site is graphically limited with very few
pictures, which could confuse text synthesisers,
and the small number of columns makes for
easier reading via Braille terminals or through
text-to-voice synthesis. The text on the home
page itself can be increased or decreased
in size with the click of a button, important
functionality for anyone with limited vision.

The simple rules followed in this site could easily
be adopted by all sites, particularly those heavy
with content. Unfortunately, many sites opt for
over-complicated methods of presenting their
information, something that can essentially make
browsing aides for the less able, redundant.

Current ALA: Eric Meyer on Print Style Sheets
Current Interview: SitePoint

16 May 2002
[1 pm | 10 am]
Newly added to the Exit Gallery, two fine sites by
Todd Dominey: Dominey Design, a distinctive and
charming professional services site crafted in Flash; and
What Do I Know, an elegantly designed and
intelligently written daily site built with XHTML and
CSS. We've linked to these sites before, but they'll be
easier to find now.

Also added to the Exit Gallery: Brainstorms & Raves,
Shirley E. Kaiser's near-daily column about web design

<les mise: old: if the great movies had been websites>

## if the great movies had been websites

Nobody loves the Web more than we do. But we're not blind to its
shortcomings. IPO Fever. Browser incompatibilities. Horrific design on a
global scale.

But that's not the worst of it.
The worst of it is the pathetic scarcity of meaningful content.
And what do many Web creators substitute for content? Diary
entries.

We'll admit we've seen a few sites that raise this kind of narcissism to
an art form. But these great personal storytelling sites are the rare
exceptions. For the most part, we get dull personal commentary with a
side order of self-importance.
Here we have the most democratic publishing medium ever invented, and what do people fill it with? The
meaningless daily details of their lives.
What if every potentially great new medium had been filled with "content" like this? What if, instead of actually
MAKING *Citizen Kane*, Orson Welles had simply published a Web diary?

**Sept. 11**
Dinner at Mankewicz's house. Mankewicz was drunk again. Had a fine porterhouse with those wonderful New England
potatoes on the side. Can't say much for the wine, but Rita seemed to like it.

**Sept. 23**
Rita appears to be bored. Complains I work too much. I told her *Citizen Kane* is going to be very important. "As
important as our love?" she said. I hate when she sounds like a cheap novel. It's exactly the kind of remark Susan,
Kane's second wife, would make. Will suggest Mankewicz work it into the screenplay.

**Sept. 25**
Ran into Cary Grant and Randolph Scott on the lot. I've heard the rumors, we all have, but Rita doesn't buy it. I think she

# USABILITY
# IS SOMETHING
# INCREDIBLY OBVIOUS

## DANNY BROWN

**EVILPUPIL**

THE EVIL THAT KIDZ DO

## 2.4 USABILITY AND THE CREATIVE SPECTRUM

**Amazon.co.uk**
Amazon has long been rated as the epitome of usability. It does exactly what it is meant to and it does it well. Few would disagree that if you want to buy a book quickly and easily online, then this is the place to do it. But few also disagree that here is the triumph of function over form, and aesthetes would argue, that while it works in what it does, it could be a lot prettier.

Nielsen has often been shunned by the creative community for his ideas about Web usability, but inevitably everyone has to accept that he is fundamentally correct. As anyone who connects to the Internet through their home modem will tell you, even the simplest pages with a handful of graphics take far too long to download. Those who wish to follow usability guidelines to create their online work will, for the most part, have to restrict their designs to mainly textual works with a minimum of graphics. At least until broadband access is more widely available.

Perhaps this is why Nielsen has rated <u>Amazon.com</u> as one of the world's most usable websites. But anyone with any kind of creative blood will tell you, Amazon is a prime example of function over form, completely practical and serving its purpose most would say, very well. But is it aesthetic? Not really.

At the other end of the spectrum come those sites that put form first and function later, perhaps to the extent where the function is a little harder to decipher. Take <u>Hell.com</u> for instance. If you do manage to be granted access, Hell.com can be a baffling place to be. Navigation can be confusing and disorientating, and the imagery held within is often far from pleasing to the eye. But this seems to be the point, and as the founder, Kenneth Aronson, explains, this is one experience that lets the user make up their own mind.

# WWW.HELL.COM

CASE STUDY// DESIGN.VARIOUS CONTRIBUTORS // SOFTWARE.HTML / FLASH

Not so much a site as a community, Hell.com makes it clear from the start that the URL has nothing to do with the occult, religion, evil or indeed any existing notion of hell. What is here is a collection of works created, controlled and maintained by its contributors, in a way that seems to defy any existing conventions of the Web or indeed design.

Once into the site (visitors have to apply to be put on the guestlist before being granted access) the experience that follows is confusing, unexpected and rarely the same twice. Essentially there

is no beginning, middle or end to the journey through Hell.com, and instead visitors interact with a series of disorientating works, moving randomly from one to the next with no foreseeable explanation, or ending, in sight.

Hell.com requires a leap of faith. Those who create for it don't have a coherent explanation of what's going on here, and all that they ask is that you don't try too hard to work it out yourself. Simply make of it what you will, and don't worry if it's not as slick and smooth as the latest commercial site you've visited.

Usability experts would be pulling their hair out if they visited this site. There seems to be no simple way of navigating it, and trying to get back to where you've just been is nigh on impossible. But that's the way it is supposed to be, and in a way it can be argued that this is representative of the Internet in general – it is a mishmash of ideas all in one place, and once out of it most users will be sure they haven't seen it all, though many will agree that they've seen enough.

//VISITORS INTERACT WITH A SERIES OF DISORIENTATING
WORKS, MOVING RANDOMLY FROM ONE TO THE NEXT

//DON'T WORRY IF IT'S NOT AS SLICK AND SMOOTH
AS THE LATEST COMMERCIAL SITE YOU'VE VISITED

"Our goal is not only non-apparent, but it's also impossible to ascertain," says Aronson. Everybody who contributes has his or her own motive for being involved. Some have very specific targets and goals, and some people have no goals whatsoever."

Hell.com seems to put to one side established themes; design values and structures, and simply does what it wants to do. Whatever the experience becomes for the individual user, there is little doubt that it probably breaks all accepted usability guidelines.

So from these two extremes of form over function and vice-versa, there must be a middle ground to the spectrum. Indeed most creative Web designers would want people to be able to fully explore their work, and so usability is fundamental. Some even go so far as to toy with usability, making it part and parcel of the user's experience.

Evilpupil.com by Yohan Gringras is one such example. To get into the site itself, one must work out a code that relates to sounds and key presses. This little challenge is not as easy for the user as a simple "click here to enter" hyperlink, but enriches the creative experience and involves the user more fully into the site, particularly with the use of sound as well as images.

**OUR GOAL IS NOT ONLY NON-APPARENT, BUT IT'S ALSO IMPOSSIBLE TO ASCERTAIN**

KENNETH ARONSON

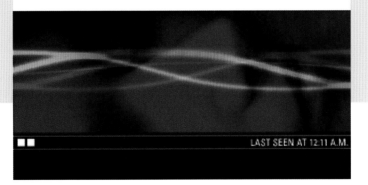

LAST SEEN AT 12:11 A.M.

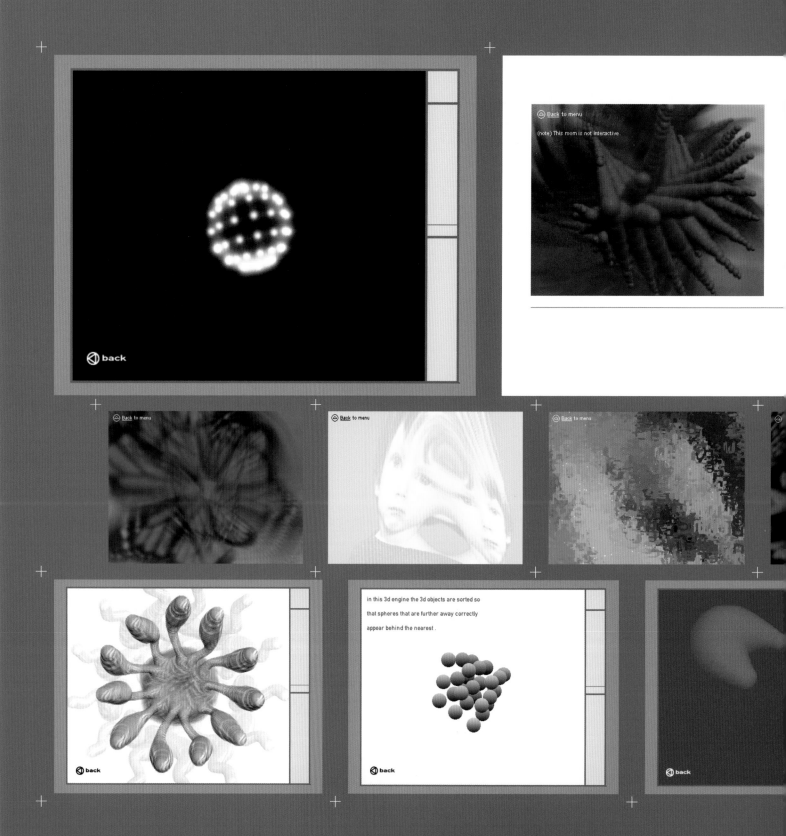

**//IT'S A PSYCHEDELIC TRIPPED OUT EXPERIENCE** DANNY BROWN

# WWW.NOODLEBOX.COM
## CASE STUDY// DESIGN.DANNY BROWN // SOFTWARE.MACROMEDIA SHOCKWAVE

Danny Brown's Noodlebox is a space for his experiments in Macromedia Shockwave and a quick glance will tell anyone that it follows the first rule of usability – it's been kept simple.

Users can access all of his works via a conventional series of hypertext links. Older works are split into many sections accessible through a graphical system, which would be quite difficult to navigate were it not for reminders of where one has and has not been. Newer works, entitled Bits and Pieces, are accessed through a visually atmospheric menu system that is intuitive and pleasing to use.

While many usability specialists would warn Web designers away from using anything other than simple HTML, Brown has kept file size to a minimum and experiments load quickly even over a slower home connection. What remains is an ambient and visually pleasing site that keeps users engaged as they create patterns and watch mathematical equations come to life in pleasant hues and organic shapes.

Brown is unashamedly proud of his work, but also proud of the level of usability it displays. He says: "One of my aims with Bits and Pieces was to be experimental, but still within parameters usable. Even though it's a psychedelic tripped out experience, I simply maintain on each screen a standard – links underlined, a description of what's going on and so on. On any page the user therefore knows what they can do, and immediately how to get back. I think it serves as a nice example of creativity and usability working well together."

Bits and Pieces

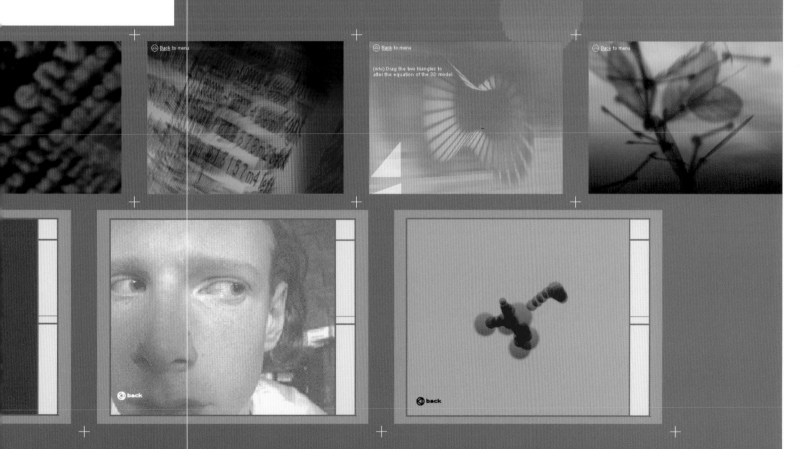

## WEB DESIGNERS ARE ONLY SHOWING THEIR OWN STUPIDITY BY SUGGESTING USABILITY SHOULD BE THROWN AWAY

DANNY BROWN

At a more fundamental level is Danny Brown's Noodlebox.com (below). Existing usability protocols of underlined text hyperlinks lead users to Brown's Shockwave experiments, where they are free to play around to their hearts' content with the interactive art and its many visual effects. Indeed, Brown believes that understanding usability is one of the fundamental aspects of understanding designing for the Web, and believes that those who ignore it are guilty of not properly addressing their own responsibilities.

"Usability is something incredibly obvious," he says. "So obvious in fact that it only goes to shame this industry that it isn't inherently part of the practice anyway. It's understandable that it took a few years to formalise, and ironically most other fields of design only matured at the same time. But now it's a fact of life, and Web designers are only showing their own stupidity by suggesting usability should be thrown away."

(info) Click-drag the mouse to draw trails.

NEED THE EVIL/PUPIL LAND MAP
(YES) // (NO)

**EVILPUPIL**
THE EVIL THAT KIDZ DO V.4.0

02

SEEN AT 11:38 P.M.

SEEN AT 11:38 P.M.

LAST SEEN AT 12:11 A.M.

LAST SEEN AT 12:11 A.M.

SEEN AT 11:35 P.M.

SEEN AT 11:35 P.M.

SHE WAS THE HIGH-SCHOOL QUEEN. A SHINY STAR FALLING TO EARTH AT 500 MILES PER HOUR. I WAS AMAZED. SHE WAS ALWAYS STONED. A STRANGE LOVE STORY, WHERE I WAS UNABLE TO TAKE SPEED NEEDED TO FLY AS FAST AS HER. I STILL REMEMBER...

Evil Pupil is subtitled "the evil that kidz do", and this sets the scene for a site that is dark, moody and mysterious. Accessing Evil Pupil is not as straightforward as ordering a book on Amazon.com, but it is not intended to be. Upon loading the initial splash page, users are given musical and textual clues as to the way forward, and only by repeating the tones they have heard using the different letters on the keyboard, can they access what lies within.

Beyond the start page, there is no traditional menu system, simply a grid of pictures which lead through to darker and more mysterious Flash movies, with sound clips accompanying images and animation that can be viewed on their own or toyed with by the user. While Evil Pupil seems to have no express function, its form is clean-cut, extremely creative, and also playful. Only by engaging with Yohan Gringras' twisted usability can one receive any gratification. Frustrating as this may be at first, clues and help is available if needed, but the reward is certainly worthy of the effort.

//ITS FORM IS CLEAN-CUT,
EXTREMELY CREATIVE, AND ALSO PLAYFUL

LARGE SWATHES OF
THEIR POTENTIAL
AUDIENCES
ESSENTIALLY
DISAPPEAR BECAUSE
THEY CANNOT GAIN
ACCESS TO THEIR
PRECIOUS WORKS OF
ELECTRONIC ART

## 2.5 TECHNOLOGICAL CONSIDERATIONS – A FOOTNOTE

Before the now commonplace use of Flash, Shockwave and Director, much of the Web followed the same format. This meant, at a most fundamental level, pages linked together with textual hyperlinks that were underlined and generally a different colour from the rest of the text on the page.

But with the development and widespread acceptance of such tools as Shockwave and Flash, these conventions no longer existed. These new graphical languages meant that anything could be a link, and unless it was made obvious by the designer, it may not be completely apparent for users to know where they should be clicking with their mice. This adds further pressures for designers to remind themselves that they are not designing for other designers, but for an audience that may not be as technically fluent as they are.

Different browsers and different computers also pose different challenges for designers, as many read the Web differently, and have different pros and cons when it comes to handling different types of media.

These combined with the old favourite that is connection speed mean it is fundamental that designers plan and then test their sites as much and as thoroughly as possible, and with as many different user groups as possible. Failure to do so may mean that large swathes of their potential audiences essentially disappear because they cannot gain access to their precious works of electronic art.

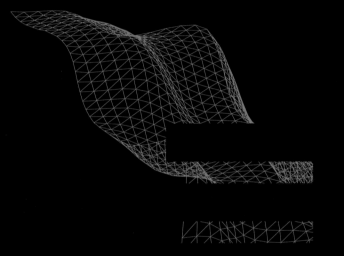
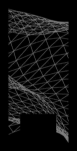
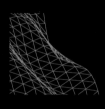

# CULTURE// <sup>72DPI</sup>

[070 KB OF 144 KB, 23KB/SEC]

# PEOPLE WHO WOULD PERHAPS HAVE NEVER BOTHERED ARE NOW FINDING IT EASY TO GET INVOLVED

ANDREW JOHNSTONE

## WITH A CLICK OF A LINK PEOPLE FROM ALL OVER THE WORLD CAN BE CHECKING OUT WHAT YOU HAVE CREATED

ANDREW JOHNSTONE

Surf the Web and you cannot avoid a vast volume of content, both textual and visual, created by individuals or groups wishing to express themselves creatively. Today, the Web is the first choice for many looking for culture, and many who wish to create culture. Whether this be to publish their own stories online, display pictures of their family, share their lives with the world, or be artistic, millions of people are turning to the Web to share themselves with the rest of the planet.

"It is so easy to have your own space on the Web," says Andrew Johnstone, creator of the popular Australian design portal, Design is Kinky. "A domain and hosting is not that expensive and that's all you really need to make a start. Doing similar things in print or video would just be way too expensive to the average designer. It is also so much easier to access a wider audience. With a click of a link people from all over the world can be checking out what you have created which is pretty much impossible in any other medium. I think this is one of the great things about the Internet because people who would perhaps have never bothered are now finding it easy to get involved."

It is this ease of use that has meant that whatever you are interested in, you can find like-minded individuals out there. And for talented creatives, this couldn't be more true.

VOLUMEONE.ISSUE.TWENTY    ENTER
PROJECTS . PRODUCTS . SEASONS

V1 ISSUE TWENTY T-SHIRT

For this issue, we have made
volumeone season 20 t-shirts.
They are 5 colors on dark grey
cotton t-shirts and feature
the go-cart graphic from the
currrent season.

CODEX SERIES THREE

The new issue of Codex is out
featuring 14 projects by Rinzen,
Develop Industrial, Dect, Elixir
Studio, Mike Young, K10K,
Charles Wilkin, Norm, The OFP
and much much more!

volumeone

AUTUMN

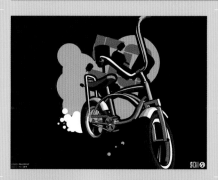

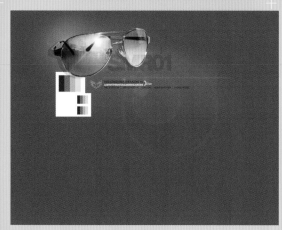

エレベーター
化粧室

springhygiene

volumeone

# WWW.VOLUMEONE.COM
## CASE STUDY// DESIGN.MATT OWENS // SOFTWARE.MACROMEDIA FLASH

Matt Owens, a Texan by origin, graduated in graphic design from the Cranbrook Academy of Art in 1995. From here he went on to become creative director and Web developer at MethodFive before setting up the Volumeone design studio in 1997. Two years later he moved on to set up the One9ine creative agency with Warren Corbitt.

Volumeone remains the laboratory of Owens' experiments in Flash and, updated seasonally, it explores four conceptual Web "narratives" that take full advantage of the latest Flash capabilities.

He sums up his work by explaining that it is "an ongoing examination/conversation between the dynamics and interrelationships of personal exploration and professional practice."

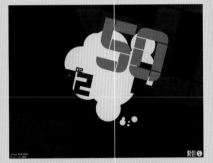

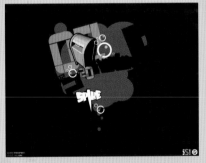

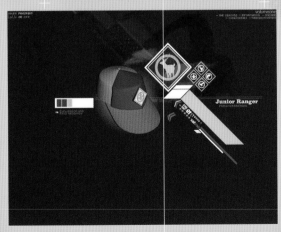

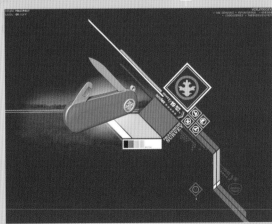

## 3.1 THE ONLINE COMMUNITY

So addictive is the Web, so satisfying the results of experimenting
with its interactivity, that there are now literally thousands of groups
and individuals who have taken their art and design online, and have
engineered it to create visual, aural and interactive experiences.
It is no surprise then, that those most prolific and most respected
within this field have become known to each other and their peers,
have shared their work and have even come together to discuss it.

While not simply content to publish work on the Web, there are also
places on the Internet where interested parties can go to learn about
new sites, exciting news and events within the design arena and even
to enter into heated debates about issues pertaining to the work they do.
These sites, or portals, have strengthened the sense of community, have
brought individuals together to share their ideas and techniques and
have worked to popularise this form of Web publishing. Even when
in-fighting does occur, the outcome is more often than not one that
adds experience and maturity to the area.

"The creative community online is more often than not very positive
and productive," explains Matt Owens of Volumeone.com. "More than
anything, it has made the creative landscape both global and intimate
which I think is its best attribute. Like any community, it can be very
inclusive and segregated but I think this is more of a by-product and
not a central intention."

PEOPLE MAKE IT OUT TO BE LIKE THIS "HELPING" ENVIRONMENT, LIKE WE ARE ALL A BUNCH OF HIPPIES MOVING TOWARDS ONE GOAL

MIKE CINA

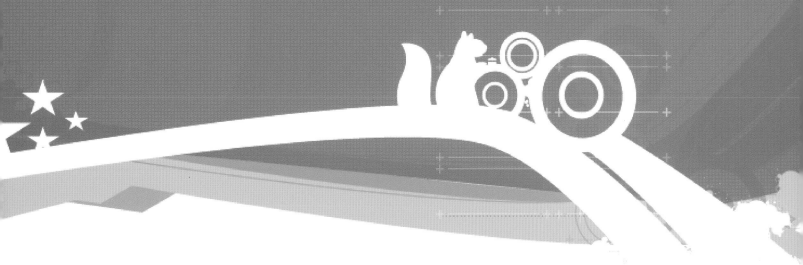

# WWW.DESIGNISKINKY.NET

CASE STUDY// DESIGN.ANDREW JOHNSTONE // SOFTWARE.VARIOUS

Design is Kinky (DiK) was created by Andrew Johnstone initially out of fun. The Australia-based designer was inspired to get on the Web in order to communicate and keep in touch with friends in other countries, but then he stumbled on to a very small design community and discovered the desire to get involved.

"I created DiK to be a part of the community, and to add something to it at the same time," he comments.

Created mainly in Adobe Photoshop, Adobe Illustrator and Macromedia Dreamweaver, his site has become one of the most popular design portals on the Web. He believes that these community sites keep people interested in what the Web can offer in terms of design, and believes that, at times, they can even be educational.

"I think people appreciate seeing this kind of content amongst the masses of portfolio sites out there that don't really do much other than promote the individual."

**I CREATED DiK TO BE A PART OF THE COMMUNITY, AND TO ADD SOMETHING TO IT AT THE SAME TIME**

ANDREW JOHNSTONE

This global intimacy that Owens talks about can occasionally be seen as closed-off and unwelcoming to many who wish to be involved (see 3.2), but generally it is considered to be a driving force, pushing design to new concepts and horizons. But often, as this driving force accelerates experimentation, these new concepts and horizons die out almost as quickly as they are born.

"Global trends and styles that are developed and propagated through the Web evolve much more quickly and have a shorter life span," says Owens.

The discussions and debates about these issues and ideas are well known for becoming heated and, on occasion, aggressive. When the new economy bubble burst in the late 1990s, such was the frustration and despair amongst many in this community, particularly those who made their living from this kind of work, that this so-called community became remarkably hostile. After a while some key sites were taken down while the situation cooled, and many lost the sense of community, even to the point that they questioned whether there was such a thing.

**GLOBAL TRENDS AND STYLES THAT ARE DEVELOPED AND PROPAGATED THROUGH THE WEB EVOLVE MUCH MORE QUICKLY AND HAVE A SHORTER LIFE SPAN**

MATT OWENS

Mike Cina, highly respected designer of TrueisTrue.com and part of WeWorkForThem.com, reflects upon the changes that occurred when things started to turn sour. He says: "People were working together, talking and working on things. But I don't see all this design community thing like it was back then. I just don't see a community. People talk about a community but I don't know if you can show me one. I wish someone would."

He adds: "The design community may be a community of people with common interests, but that is as far as I would go. People make it out to be like this 'helping' environment, like we are all a bunch of hippies moving towards one goal. There are some great designers out there helping people which is great. But I see it as a bunch of people that like doing their own thing."

Perhaps the real blow that shook everyone in the community when the Web's most popular design portal, Kaliber10000 (www.k10k.net), closed its doors to the many hundreds of thousands of design centric users who visited it each day. In the last email newsletter to its loyal followers before it went on extended vacation to redesign, refresh and regroup, Michael Schmidt and Toke Nygaard proclaimed: "The last year has been nasty. There's been tremendous unrest in the so-called 'design community', and we are sick and tired of constantly being blamed for everything that's wrong with the current state of design." Then they went on holiday to refresh themselves and redesign their site.

**www.db-db.com**
Hong Kong-based Francis
Lam runs the design
portal Db-db. Subtitled
"our design playground",
initial entrance to the
site takes the form of
a chat environment,
with everyone connected
represented by small
pixel-sized characters.
Here they can talk about
issues one-to-one with
other users, or in a
group for all to see.

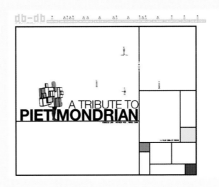

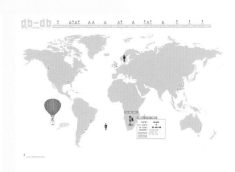

Delving further into the
site takes the user
to a more conventional
screen, still populated
by the same pixel-sized
characters and still
with the same chat
functionality. But the
background instead
tells of design news,
links to interviews with
key members of the
community, details of

relevant events, and
the now customary
news stream with links
to recent stories and
sites. Lam's personal
projects are also
available for perusal,
and the site as a whole
joins the dots around
the pacific rim, adding
a mature, more global
perspective to the
design community.

THE ONLY REASON
THE POPULAR PEOPLE
ARE POPULAR IS
BECAUSE THEY HAVE
DONE THE HARD WORK
AND GOT INVOLVED

ANDREW JOHNSTONE

## 3.2 SAVIOURS OF DESIGN
## OR ELITIST KILLERS OF ORIGINALITY?

Many of the design portals allow certain users to post comments about design, links to interesting websites and generally encourage discussion about the state of the online design scene. However, very few of these sites are open to the general public, and generally those who add their insight into design are usually invited guests or friends of the site designers. And this has raised certain questions about the validity and function of what these sites aim to do.

Critics claim that such an insular environment where no new voices are heard, and where the same voices share ideas, creates an air of elitism. Beyond this, many believe that the lack of a new perspective prohibits originality, instead forcing design around in circles.

Andrew Johnstone comments: "I do think this can happen and I think that it has been the downfall of a few portals over the last few years. But what people need to understand is that when individuals get a bit of popularity in the scene they tend to communicate a little bit more with other popular people and therefore when starting a new project they will ask these people to join them. This then can look elitist when that was not the intention at all."

# WWW.THREEOH.COM
## CASE STUDY// DESIGN.JAMES WIDEGREN // SOFTWARE.HTML

ThreeOh was created by James Widegren and a selection of his friends to highlight the best in Web design. Like most portal and community sites it has a regularly updated news section, bringing attention to new sites and experiments and events, and also provides profiles of designers and features on interesting issues and subjects.

ThreeOh, is also the originator of the May 1st Reboot contest (www.may1reboot.com) in which people are invited to close down their own sites around the middle of April, and redesign them. They are then relaunched on the first of May. The contest is subtitled "a reinvigoration of the Web."

# //A REINVIGORATION OF THE WEB

# WWW.DPLANET.ORG
**CASE STUDY// DESIGN.DAMIAN STEPHENS // SOFTWARE.HTML**

South African based Damian Stephens runs Dplanet in his spare time between being CEO of No Organisation and working with agencies such as Type01. The site includes features relevant to design issues, interviews with leading names in the field, and also several community elements, such as the Cycle.occur, which allows people to upload their own images or Flash animation. Cycle.occur is uncensored and relies on the discipline of those taking part to restrict what they upload, and also acts as inspiration to others who wish to observe this evolving and never static project.

Within the creative community there are names that will occur time and time again, that become familiar. These names are of those who work tirelessly to push their design, their use of the technology and experimentation of ideas further and further, and in doing so they become recognised and either receive commendation or criticism from the rest of the community. But either way, they are moving it forward, evoking debate and motivating others to either work on their ideas, or correct their wrongs, depending on the individual's opinion.

Johnstone adds: "If people are annoyed at seeing the same 'big names' on these sites it is usually just because the 'big names' are willing to get involved. The only reason the popular people are popular is because they have done the hard work and got involved."

**WHEN INDIVIDUALS GET A BIT OF POPULARITY IN THE SCENE THEY TEND TO COMMUNICATE A LITTLE BIT MORE WITH OTHER POPULAR PEOPLE AND THEREFORE WHEN STARTING A NEW PROJECT THEY WILL ASK THESE PEOPLE TO JOIN THEM. THIS THEN CAN LOOK ELITIST WHEN THAT WAS NOT THE INTENTION AT ALL**

ANDREW JOHNSTONE

Alt.sense is a community site in the sense that anyone is free to post their own comments and read what others have said. Naude, however, maintains that the site "is not a bulletin board", and its main purpose is an experimental playground, where he can publish his latest design projects and essays relevant to the design community and industry.

## numer.02

INTRODUCTION - LOOK AHEAD
PROCESS AND ADEQUACY
INTERACTIVE CINEMA
PERFORMANCES

19

INTERACTION DESIGN - LOOK AHEAD
APRIL 2002, CENTRE POMPIDOU, PARIS

2002-05-11 00:32:03     dplanet::

Interesting introduction to media activism from a Palestinian perspective at Electronic Intifada

2002-05-06 08:14:07     //alt.sense

[ Personal Update or At last I'm online again!]

Hello everyone! In a couple of years, I will refer to the past four weeks as "A Significant Period". Hopefully I would've forgotten the hurry of every breathing hour, and sit quietly on my balcony in confirmation of all the good things I am anticipating.

Before leaving for Numer.02 [ 17 April ], I resigned from type01 with effect from 1 May. The studio at Roeland Square has been my home for four years; when the decision was made to move type01 to The Foundry, I realised that it is also time for me to sort through my past and create a new, independant environment for myself from all the good things I experienced and look forward to doing.

This alone could justify my "Significant Period", but my visit to Europe for numer.02 contributed greatly to the inspiration for my bright outlook on the way forward. I have met so many beautiful people during the conference who said so much of importance and value, that I am busy writing a numer.02_report to post seperately to this general update. I've taken many photographs at numer.02 as well and will post them soon. So, be a bit more patient for that numer.02 feedback:) In the meantime, massive thanks to Pierre, Sara, Halory and everyone else who organised this significantly sweet event!

Although I was floating around with terrible flu, it was wonderful to see Petra, Jake and Eduard in Rotterdam again!!! Sorry I couldn't be there for Shine guys :(( Because of said flu, most of my time in the Netherlands was spent in bed in Den Hague. A city that is host to some wonderful people, such as Thomas from lust, Tomak [ sp? ] at locale.01, Peter from Dumbar and Peter from Idis. But most wonderful of all was the beautiful apartment in Paviljoensgracht where I was given a home by two dear friends, Johanna and Peter. I had a special time with you two and miss you much!

Despite a great time in Europe, I was happy to come back to Cape Town. So the cocky chap at customs irritated my nicotine-nervous system, but the cheese made it to the fridge and is ripe to be served. I have so much things that needs to be done now that I'm back home, but there is a new rush of inspirational adrenalin that still throws me out of bed at 7 in the morning. Damian and myself formed a partnership called no™ to allow us to work internationally on commercial and cultural projects. My studio at home is finally set up and I've started the process of getting everything organised. My inbox is next on the list, so all those who emailed me will shortly receive the long overdue reply. Those who used to get to alt.sense using altsense.com would've noticed that the .net and .com domains were seperated. I will develop altsense.com with a personal agenda, whilst continuing to develop altsense.net for use by the community. A faster host is first priority after realising how slow it is for international visitors!

And now I better post this update:)

2002-05-07 22:48:27     rollerball

Wilcofilm is an extensive site for the film "I am Trying to Break Your Heart" that chronicles Wilco's recording sessions (for the recent Yankee Hotel Foxtrot), live shows and some record label turmoil

2002-05-07 02:57:57     nekada_n.tosic

::Moby.Com::/

net.art or "great" official website?

it has everything from drawings, forum, photos and even essays on prisoners civil rights and such issues / its on of the most bizzare sites i have ever seen / i have spent a lot of time on it ( more then 10 mins which is a lot of time ) / check it out

| UPDATES | | | | |
|---|---|---|---|---|
| DISCUSSIONS | discussions | [05/10/02] | Software Piracy | dp:: |
| PROJECTS | photo.album | [05/11/02] | sweat | Dill |
| PROJECTS | postcards | [14/11/01] | + (062) | Emma Guerard |
| PROJECTS | blitz_GIF | [03/17/02] | 002 culture _//_couture | update:04.12.02 |
| LIBRARY | asci | [04/08/02] | Unlimited Photography Now! | Bill Davenport |
| LIBRARY | binary | [27/03/02] | 3 x 2 split_pix | David Wakeman |

INSTANT.POLL

[ toothpaste aesthetics ]    A     182     119     B

| ASSOCIATE ADVERT | ASSOCIATE LINK | ALT.SENSE MAILING LIST |
|---|---|---|
| WWW.URBANEXPRESS.CO.UK | | SUBSCRIBE > |

HAPPY.BIRTHDAY

11/may     ... no birthdays today ...

---

| 05 | [ blitz_GIF ] | The aim of blitz_GIF is to provide themes and showcase animations that was developed for that particular theme. Anyone is invited to participate in these explorations of the almost-forgotten animated gif. |
| 04 | [ POSTCARD.project ] | This dplanet: project aims to distribute 'collectable' physical art objects (in the form of postcards) created by members of the digital networked community (digital tourists) |
| 03 | [ instant.poll ] | This is not a discussion, but a question of [ A ] or [ B ] . Submit your opinion, but think carefully as you can do this once only. Results are non-negotiable and visible to all. |
| 02 | [ photo.album ] | A facility for the alt.sense community to share photographs by uploading them to the alt.sense server. You can create and manage your own album, post a photo to the open_album or invite people via email to visit the collections. |
| 01 | [ happy.birthday ] | Initially an experiment in information visualisation, this project continues to expand its number of participants who believe in a more personal approach to networked culture. Calendar views, birthday cards and email reminders creates a platform for interaction |

alt.sense > photo.album

[ victorybros ]

email this album to a friend

victory brother    stay high 149    untitled

msg    jest txt    a love

broader than broadway

email this album to a friend

# ALL MY SHIT
# IS OPEN SOURCE

## DAMIAN STEPHENS

### 3.3 SHARE AND SHARE ALIKE –
### AN OPEN SOURCE IDEOLOGY OF DESIGN

While arguments and debates are part of the driving force behind the online design community, there is no denying that ideas and inspirations are communicated and shared between designers and experimenters and innovators alike. But this sharing idea goes a lot further than simple communication.

Open source, the idea of allowing anyone to access and use the codes from your Flash experiments, the engineering behind your designs and interactivities, is a fundamental theme behind the online community. This ideology, though not shared by all, moves forward the development of new concepts in interaction design by allowing others to take further your experimentation where you have let it rest, and lets them modify and employ it within their own designs.

Damian Stephens of Dplanet.org and No Organisation comments:
"All my shit is open source."

While the arguments about elitism and insularity are destined to go on as long as there is a design community it seems that the very presence of open source indicates to the contrary. This underlying sharing of technologies and work cannot but emphasise and reinforce the fact that, while on the outside it may seem about who is producing the best work, who can get their name into the minds of their peers, and who can win what appears to be a contest, this is a community of egalitarianism, based on sharing, communicating and helping others to develop their own skills.

**OPEN SOURCE, THE IDEA OF ALLOWING ANYONE TO ACCESS AND USE THE CODES FROM YOUR FLASH EXPERIMENTS, THE ENGINEERING BEHIND YOUR DESIGNS AND INTERACTIVITIES, IS A FUNDAMENTAL THEME BEHIND THE ONLINE COMMUNITY**

# WWW.PRATE.COM
## CASE STUDY// DESIGN.JEMMA GURA

Prate (www.prate.com) and Precinct (www.precinct.com) are projects run by Jemma Gura and Daniel Achilles respectively. They are blank canvasses where the designers publish their art, toy with Flash creations, and present to the world their own work in progress and they play around with new ideas, concepts and themes. Sometimes aesthetically pleasing and even beautiful, other times jarring and awkward, both these sites provide a fresh look at visual devices online.

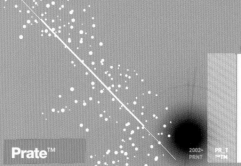

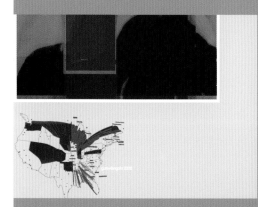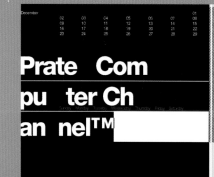

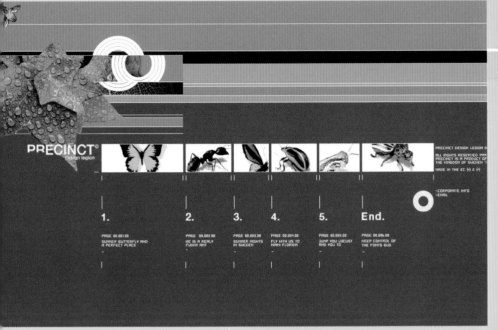

## //BOTH THESE SITES PROVIDE A FRESH LOOK AT VISUAL DEVICES ONLINE

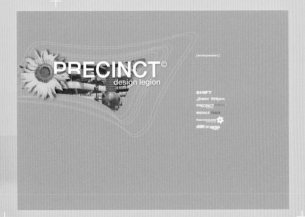

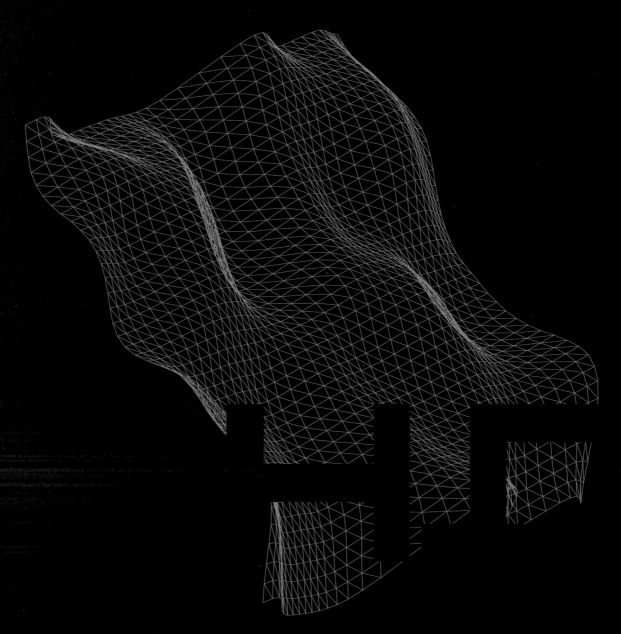

# TECHNOLOGY// <sup>72DPI</sup>

[092 KB OF 144 KB, 23KB/SEC]

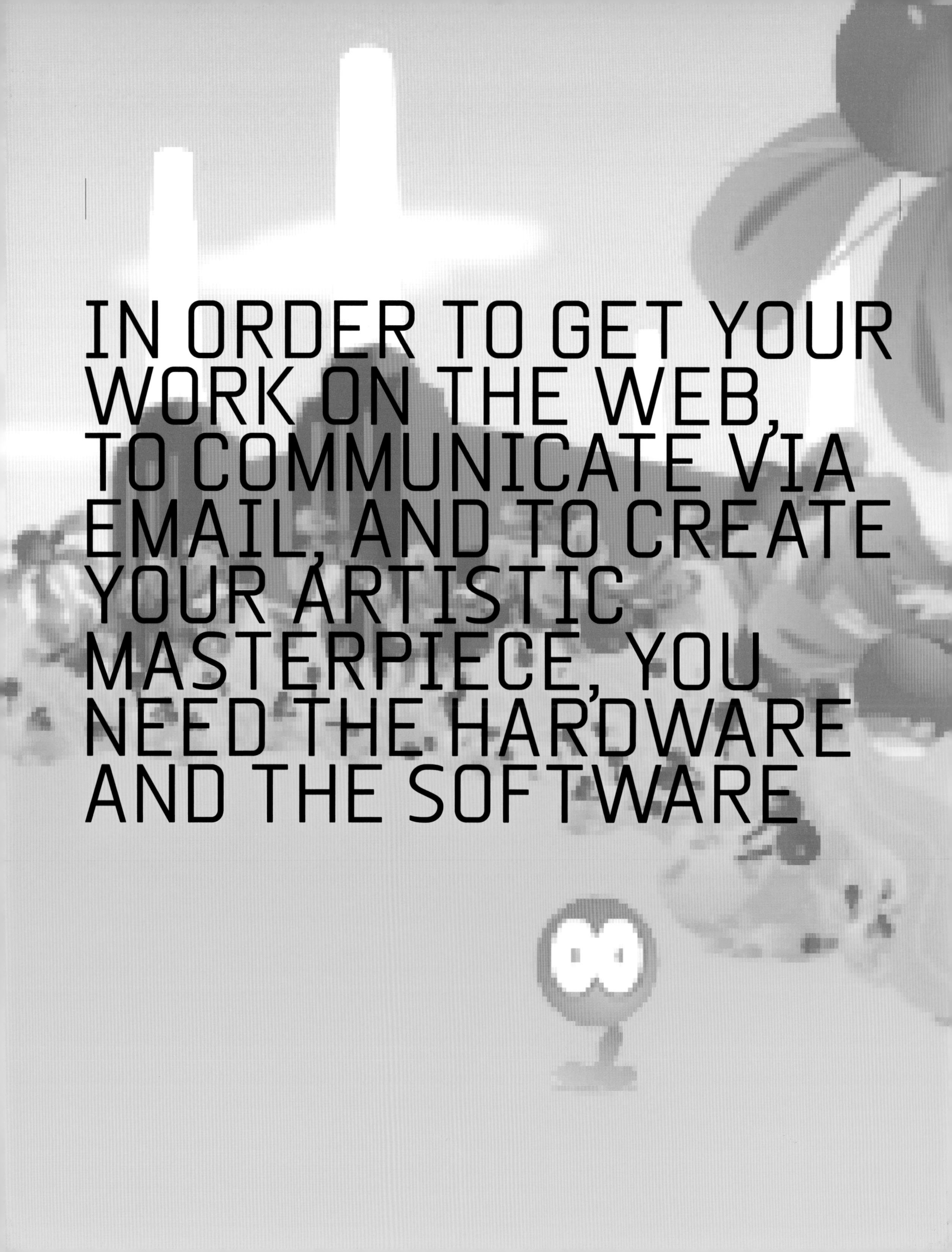

IN ORDER TO GET YOUR
WORK ON THE WEB,
TO COMMUNICATE VIA
EMAIL, AND TO CREATE
YOUR ARTISTIC
MASTERPIECE, YOU
NEED THE HARDWARE
AND THE SOFTWARE

Since the inception of the World Wide Web, the main focus of the attention it received was based on the potential and the possibilities that it held. There was the freedom of speech that it could provide to everybody who was interested, the possibility of getting your work to the world without the need for an intermediate publisher. In short, it had become an egalitarian machine that gave the individual the same power as the multinational conglomerate.

But in order to get your work on the Web, to communicate via email, and to create your artistic masterpiece, you need the hardware and the software. Anybody who wishes to get connected must have some means to do it, and in the early days of home computer, the initial cost was similar to that of purchasing a small car. So the great equaliser that it promised to be was still a long way off.

But as home computing took off, and as generation after generation of new devices came to be, the computer became another part of the disposable society. In major cities around the world, you don't have to go far to find hardware thrown into the trash, ready to be picked up by anybody who passes by. While these machines may not run as quickly or as reliably as the latest models, it is still sufficient in order to get connected and start creating for the masses.

Indeed, the actual technology required to access and host Web pages is incredibly small. It is even possible to create a Web server little larger than a matchbox. With a little know how, and a little ingenuity, almost anybody can get connected, get creating, and get their work to the world.

## 4.1 THE HARDWARE

It is generally accepted that to get online you need a PC or an Apple Mac computer. Brand new, these can cost into the thousands, but you don't have to look further than the small ads of the local paper to find computers that, while still perfectly capable of creating for, and surfing the Web, are generally undesirable and considered worthless.

But connected technology doesn't stop there. Today there is a whole host of technology that not only connects to, but also can be used to create for the Web. In the UK, Amstrad has produced the "Emailer", what appears to be a glorified telephone answering machine that can send email, SMS text messages and even browse selected websites. Some cable and satellite television packages allow you to do the same, and interactive television (iTV) goes further, with some companies, such as banks and even fast-food producers, creating services tailored specifically to this new medium.

But the advances in mobile wireless technology have made the real difference in this area. Portable computers, such as the Pocket PC and Palm Pilot can now, when paired with a cell phone or a wireless plug-in adapter be used to access the Internet. Pocket PCs in particular, many of which run on a scaled down version of Microsoft Windows can be used to create content, provide design and generally update your site.

**TODAY THERE IS A WHOLE HOST OF TECHNOLOGY THAT NOT ONLY CONNECTS TO, BUT ALSO CAN BE USED TO CREATE FOR THE WEB**

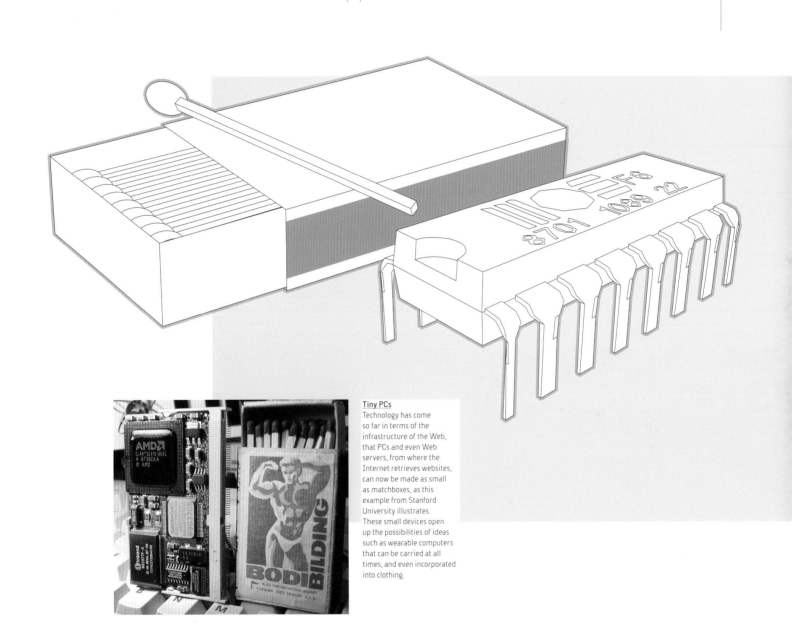

### Tiny PCs

Technology has come so far in terms of the infrastructure of the Web, that PCs and even Web servers, from where the Internet retrieves websites, can now be made as small as matchboxes, as this example from Stanford University illustrates. These small devices open up the possibilities of ideas such as wearable computers that can be carried at all times, and even incorporated into clothing.

# THE WEB TRANSITIONED FROM A SIMPLE RESOURCE TO A COMMERCIAL PROMOTIONS TOOL. THIS BALANCE BETWEEN UTILITY AND PROMOTION REMAINS AT THE FOREFRONT OF WEB DEVELOPMENT TODAY

MATT OWENS

## 4.2 HTML

HTML (Hypertext Mark-up Language) is the starting point for any designer looking to get their work on to the Web. Essentially this language tells the computer's browser how to display text: what font to use, how big it should be, what colour and where it should be placed.

But HTML also describes to the browser how, where and what size to display images at. This provides the basis for any online page layout, and though many technologies have come since it was first developed, it is still necessary in 90% of all cases, to call these other technologies into action.

But while HTML is considered by most experienced Web designers to be out of date and too basic for their needs, its simple functionality makes it ideal for anyone who wants to add interactivity to their visual creations. Images can be instructed to change when the mouse pointer passes over them, different areas within bigger images can provide links to more content and further designs, and video clips, animations and sounds can all be manipulated with this fundamental Web programming language.

The operation of HTML lies in simple tags. For example, if text is to be displayed in a bold type then the tag <B> is placed before it, and </B> after it. The same goes when creating a hyperlink. The text that is to become the link is prefixed with an <A HREF="…"> tag, where "…" is the URL of the new page to connect to, and it is suffixed by </A> to end the hyperlink.

This simplicity has meant that scores of people have taken to creating their own home pages, to the extent that there are now literally billions (no one can be sure how many to be precise) of Web pages on the net.

But although millions of people have harnessed the power of HTML to create their own sites and pages, relatively few have taken advantage of the tools to create interesting design and layouts, and as a result the Web has become, for many, an unstimulating and rather negative experience. It is these experiences that lead designers to demand much more from their Web authoring software, and in the process turned the Web from a simple global database of documents to a much more commercial entity.

"The limitations of static HTML were so boring compared to, for example, CD-ROM work," explains Matt Owens, the creator of Volumeone.com. "I think the commercial desire to engage people and hold their attention became a motivating factor in the Web's evolution. The Web transitioned from a simple resource to a commercial promotions tool. This balance between utility and promotion remains at the forefront of Web development today."

**html code**
While it may seem complicated at first glance, the basics of HTML programming are extremely easy to understand. A simple set of instructions like these (right) can be used to create pleasing results (left). It is easy to imagine what a more advanced understanding of the code could create.

*Past Present Future: Inspiring Creative Web Design*

by Chris Brock

**Published by AVA Publishing**

```
<html>
<head>
<title>Untitled Document</title>
<meta http-equiv+"Content-Type" content="text/html; charset =iso-8859-1">
</head>

<body bgcolor="#FF0033" text="#000000">
<p align="center"> </p>
<p> </p>
<p> </p>
<table width="100%" border="0" cellspacing="0" cellpadding="5">
 <tr>
  <td>
   <table width="100%" border="0" cellspacing="0" cellpadding="5">
    <tr>
     <tr>
      <div align="center"><font face="Arial, Helvetica, sans serif"
size="+7"><b><strong><em><font color="#FFFFFF">Past
       Present Future: Inspiring Creative Web
Design</font></em></strong></b></font></div>
     </td>
    </tr>
    <tr>
     <td>
      <p> </p>
      <p align="center"><font face="Geneva, Arial, Helvetica, san-serif"
size="6".<b><font color="#FFFFFF">by
       Chris Brock</font></b></font></p>
     </td>
    </tr>
    <tr>
     <td>
      <div align="center"><font face="Verdana, Arial, Helvetica, sans serif"
size="6"><b><font size+"5" color="#FFFFFF">Published
       by AVA Publishing</font></b></font></div>
     </td>
    </tr>
   </table>
  </td>
 </tr>
</table>
<p> </p>
</body>
</html>
```

### 4.3 DHTML

For many, HTML provided a taste of the potential of the Web, but they wanted more. Much more. Though Flash and Shockwave provide the ability to create much more dynamic, interactive experiences, many users, particularly those who connect to the Internet from home over a simple dial-up connection are left out, either because the Web pages are too big to be quickly downloaded, or because they do not have the appropriate software add-ons that are required.

So some designers turned to DHTML (Dynamic Hypertext Mark-up Language). As its name suggests, it is basically HTML but with added kick. With DHTML programmers and designers are able to create moving, animated user interfaces for their websites, and content that users can browse through in much more flexible and dynamic ways.

But the fundamental benefits of DHTML lie in the ease with which back-end developers can use it to their benefit. Such is the flexibility of the language that, rather than having to build all content management and database systems (for the provision of content) around the front-end interface designs, DHTML can be programmed to afford the back-end developers a system that more appropriately suites their needs. Users too, are able to manipulate the information drawn from these databases and back-end systems much more flexibly than with sites developed in Flash.

A PAGE OF FLASH IS MUCH HARDER TO PRINT, COPY, MANIPULATE AND EXTRACT TEXT FROM THAN A PAGE OF DHTML – PROVIDED THAT THE PAGE HAS BEEN BUILT WITH EASE OF USE IN MIND

SOPHIE ROCHESTER

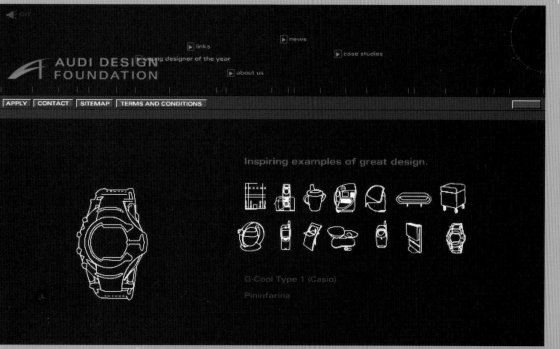

Inspiring examples of great design.

G-Cool Type 1 (Casio)
Pininfarina

APPLY | CONTACT | SITEMAP | TERMS AND CONDITIONS

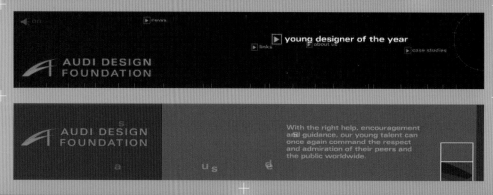

With the right help, encouragement and guidance, our young talent can once again command the respect and admiration of their peers and the public worldwide.

Inspiring examples of great design.

Neptune Advanced Communication Terminal
Keiner Dufort Design

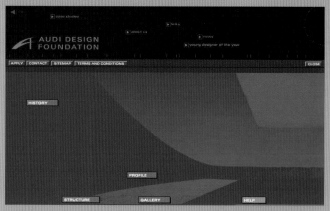

HISTORY

PROFILE

STRUCTURE    GALLERY    HELP

# WWW.AUDIFOUNDATION.CO.UK

**CASE STUDY// DESIGN.GOOD TECHNOLOGY // SOFTWARE.FLASH / DHTML / HTML**

The site that London's Good Technology created for the Audi-sponsored foundation for promoting new design talent, the Audi Foundation, was unusual in the way it used technology. On the site's home page was not only basic HTML, but also DHTML and Flash.

This somewhat unusual approach to creating a site was chosen so that the Foundation, which had a minimal staff, could update the site themselves, without the costly requirement of bringing the design agency back each time they needed to add content and information. As a result, the navigation bar at the top of the screen was created in Flash, and the bottom half of the screen, where moveable windows presented relevant information drawn from a database, was created in HTML.

"The site had to have a look that was stunning yet minimalist," explains Good Technology's Sophie Rochester. "We decided to reinvent the wheel with DHTML – to try to build a windowing system within the browser that allowed the site designer to carry out tasks in a way not supported by standard HTML."

DHTML was chosen because of its sheer flexibility when handling information from a database, and the visual look of the finished site is crisp and clean, reflecting the stylish nature of the content it presents.

There was a trade-off, however. Developing the site was extremely labour intensive, and the finished product was not completely compatible with the Netscape Navigator browser version 6, but only versions up to 4 and Microsoft's Internet Explorer.

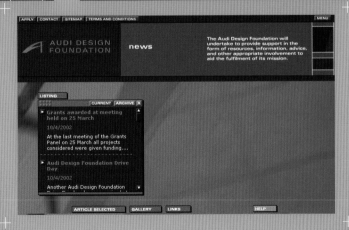

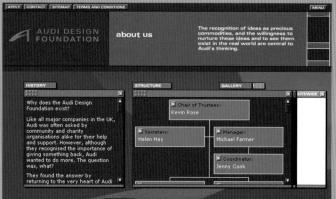

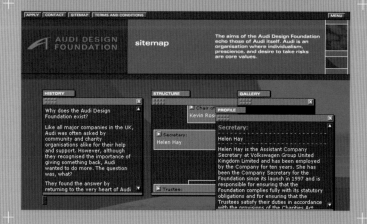

//THE SITE HAD TO HAVE A LOOK THAT
**WAS STUNNING YET MINIMALIST** SOPHIE ROCHESTER

Sophie Rochester, of the UK's agency, Good Technology, explains: "a page of Flash is much harder to print, copy, manipulate and extract text from than a page of DHTML – provided that the page has been built with ease of use in mind."

There are trade-offs, however. DHTML requires a great deal of processing on the side of the users' computer. On older machines this can slow site functions considerably, as DHTML requires far more calculations than Flash would for a similar effect. Added to this are the development and testing times, which are far longer than with most other languages. To add insult to injury it is often nearly impossible to persuade the DHTML-designed site to run on every platform available. These are all things that tend to put designers off using it.

But that doesn't mean that it won't be making a reappearance in the future. Those who do work with it believe its flexibility is the key to its success, particularly in areas such as Intranets (in-house "Internets" for corporate use) and with systems that clients wish to maintain themselves.

Rochester explains: "DHTML is derived from HTML and comes from a document mark-up/display point of view. Something like Flash is mostly to do with multi-media interactive vector-driven content where the content may play second fiddle to the style. DHTML will prove to be a VERY powerful tool for Intranets and administering content management systems as sites move toward a more client managed approach."

## DHTML WILL PROVE TO BE A VERY POWERFUL TOOL FOR INTRANETS AND ADMINISTERING CONTENT MANAGEMENT SYSTEMS AS SITES MOVE TOWARD A MORE CLIENT MANAGED APPROACH

SOPHIE ROCHESTER

# WE CHOSE FLASH BECAUSE IT ALLOWS YOU TO DEVELOP COMPLEX, DYNAMIC NAVIGATION SYSTEMS, AND DYNAMIC CONTENT APPLICATIONS NOT AFFORDED BY HTML

SOPHIE ROCHESTER

F9000 MAILING SERVICE
▶ FOR THE LATEST F9000 UPDATES SUBSCRIBE HERE

DESIGN/CONCEPT
CREATED BY GOODTECHNOL

## 4.4 PLUG-INS – MACROMEDIA FLASH

The real break for Web designers came when software company Macromedia launched Flash, essentially an animation tool, for the Web. Suddenly at their fingertips designers had the ability to make smoothly animated, quick loading, moving, interactive works for the Web. As new versions of the software became available, new functions were added increasing its functionality and turning it into a package that no longer required the works to be called into action from an HTML page.

In order to view the Flash animations, users had to have an appropriate plug-in, an additional piece of software, which would allow their browser to read and display the Flash files. At first, with slower connections, it required a hefty file downloaded from the Web which took time, and for those who were not as computer literate as others, was too complicated to handle.

But as its popularity increased, and more designers began to use the tool to create their work, it started to receive a wider acknowledgement as a must-have accompaniment to any browser. Many sites that incorporate Flash also have a plain HTML version available for those who do not have the plug-in, but this is becoming increasingly rare, particularly as it now comes as part of the package when many home computers are sold, and as more and more people become aware of its existence. It is now estimated that 97% of home computers incorporate the software, and Macromedia, as well as many Web designers, believes that eventually it will yield the death knell for HTML-based pages.

"I think flash changed the Web forever," admits Matt Owens. "It has made the Web more alive than it has ever been, and it has made it a far more organic place that is far more responsive to and a reflection of the real world."

I THINK FLASH CHANGED THE WEB FOREVER. IT HAS MADE THE WEB MORE ALIVE THAN IT HAS EVER BEEN, AND IT HAS MADE IT A FAR MORE ORGANIC PLACE THAT IS FAR MORE RESPONSIVE TO AND A REFLECTION OF THE REAL WORLD

MATT OWENS

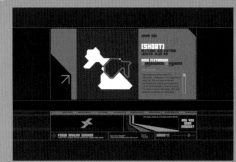

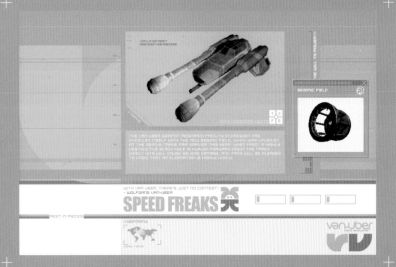

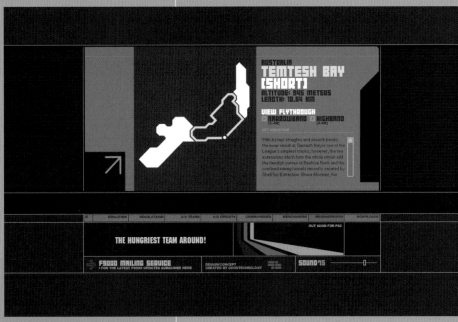

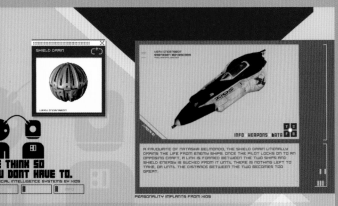

# WWW.WIPEOUTFUSION.COM

CASE STUDY// DESIGN.GOOD TECHNOLOGY // SOFTWARE.MACROMEDIA FLASH

The website for Wipeout Fusion, the popular futurist racing game for PlayStation 2, was created completely in Flash by Good Technology. Designing sites for computer games is not an easy task, as incorporating games only detracts from the product you are supposed to be promoting. So Good Technology created an online world that reflected the different teams that appear in the game.

"We chose flash because it allows you to develop complex, dynamic navigation systems, and dynamic content applications not afforded by HTML," explains Sophie Rochester. "The compromise is that it takes longer to develop in due to the scripting, but then you would expect that to be the case."

The finished site is an animated, dynamic environment with scrolling maps, impressive graphics and sounds borrowed from the game. Building on the game's already huge fan-base, the site creates a community area for players to come together, share best times and set challenges for others to beat.

Complicated 3D flythroughs of different courses were created using six different software packages, adding to the final overall quality of the game, which took a great deal of time and effort to complete, but might easily have taken more. As Rochester explains: "You can carry on refining forever. A good design job is one where you get the kind of results you wanted in the time you have."

## 4.5 PLUG-INS – MACROMEDIA SHOCKWAVE

Before they developed Flash, Macromedia launched Shockwave, which did essentially the same job, but which many designers believe is more flexible, allowing the designer to do more and create much more complex works. But as the lines between Flash and Shockwave become increasingly fuzzy, designers, and even Macromedia, are moving away from it.

Danny Brown, the creator of Noodlebox.com, works primarily in Shockwave, and can't imagine working with anything else. He says "Shockwave is now a fantastic tool. It's a fully featured, fast and easy-to-use application development tool for the Web. Yet Macromedia seems loathed to support it, and developers seem loathed to do anything interesting with it."

For many, however, Shockwave is seen more as a tool for creating interactive animations for use in, say CD-ROMs, and it doesn't support the dynamic functions that the latest versions of Flash boast. Indeed it is possible today to build not only the front-end visual interface of a site in Flash, but also the database of content behind it and even the content management system (CMS) that allows the site and its database to be updated.

# SHOCKWAVE IS NOW A FANTASTIC TOOL. IT'S A FULLY FEATURED, FAST AND EASY-TO-USE APPLICATION DEVELOPMENT TOOL FOR THE WEB

DANNY BROWN

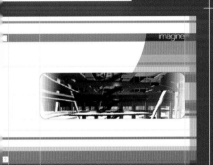

# WWW.THEPOWERSTATION.CO.UK

CASE STUDY// DESIGN.RANDOM MEDIA // SOFTWARE.MACROMEDIA SHOCKWAVE

Thepowerstation.co.uk was created by the UK's Random Media for Parkview International London PLC, the company behind the redevelopment of London's Battersea Power Station. At the time the actual plan to develop the power station had not properly been formed so the site was created to give a taste of the potential of one of the city's most famous landmarks.

Random Media's Victor Benady explains: "We wanted to produce a taster site that provides an emotional experience to users. We wanted users to feel the excitement of the core values that the power station project embodies. All this needed to be done without giving too much away."

Random Media decided to use Shockwave rather than Flash on this site because they felt that what they might have done in Flash could be done much more gracefully in Shockwave. Developing the site in Shockwave also meant that it would run faster on the average user's machine.

Incorporating eight interactive environments, or "moodscapes", the site takes the user on a journey that creates an atmospheric experience and provides a glimpse of the building's future. Games, animations and multi-user areas all add up to create a visually stunning site that only enhances the building's already familiar shape and personality.

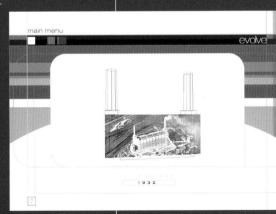

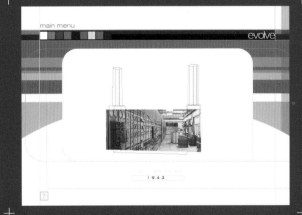

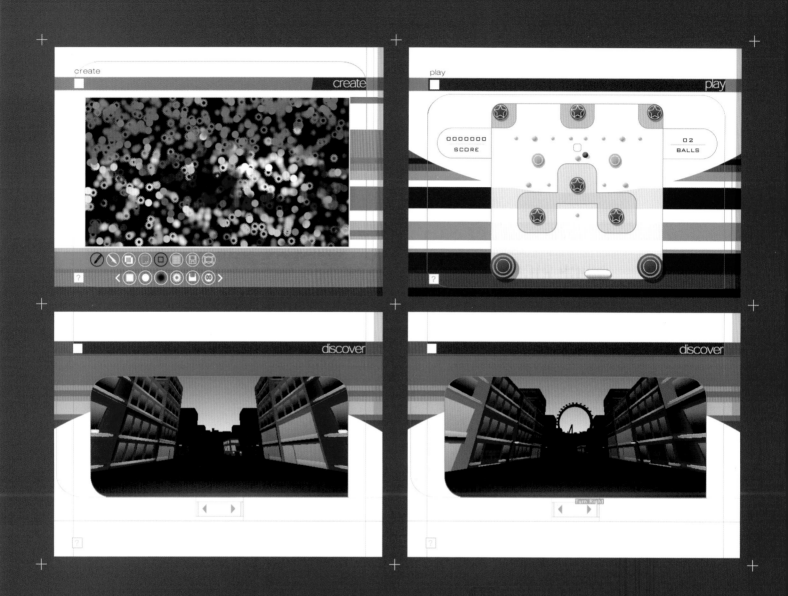

//GAMES, ANIMATIONS AND MULTI-USER AREAS ALL ADD UP
TO CREATE A VISUALLY STUNNING SITE THAT ONLY ENHANCES
THE BUILDING'S ALREADY FAMILIAR SHAPE AND PERSONALITY

**ALTHOUGH THE GAP IS CLOSING BETWEEN FLASH AND SHOCKWAVE, SHOCKWAVE STILL PROVIDES A MUCH RICHER EXPERIENCE AND GIVEN THE INCREASE IN BROADBAND I THINK SHOCKWAVE WILL HAVE ITS DAY ONCE AGAIN**

VICTOR BENADY

However, it may not necessarily be the end of Shockwave as we know it. As broadband gains popularity, particularly in the UK and the USA, Shockwave is making a comeback that many didn't expect. New features such as 3D capability are enticing many users to look at the software once again.

"I think Shockwave's future lies in the broadband arena," explains Victor Benady, creative director at the London-based studio, Random Media. "Although the gap is closing between Flash and Shockwave, Shockwave still provides a much richer experience and given the increase in broadband I think Shockwave will have its day once again. The recently added 3D features are useful, particularly for games, but I think this development is a bit of a red herring in the wider context of Shockwave's potential."

Benady is a fan of Shockwave, not least because in many of the areas that Flash fails, Shockwave comes shining through. He says: "The high number of calculations required to make rich vector-based animation and interactivity work can mean that Flash crawls on slower hardware. Shockwave provides a much more fluid and impactful experience."

## 4.6 PLUG-INS – ADOBE ATMOSPHERE

In 2001 Adobe, famous for its design software such as Photoshop, Illustrator and Acrobat, launched Atmosphere. The intention was to grab back a market that it was losing to Macromedia, who were applying tools to products such as Flash and Shockwave that could potentially have made the need for Adobe software redundant. It hoped that Atmosphere was going to be the next step after Flash, and would steer the field of interactive design in a new direction. But to date, this hasn't been the case.

Atmosphere is a tool for creating 3D environments that users can explore from a first-person perspective. With Atmosphere, websites can be designed like a house – with users moving from room to room, and in each room is a different section of the site, a new piece of information or a new interactive experience to be enjoyed.

**FADS FOR 3D NAVIGATION SYSTEMS COME AND GO, BUT THE REALITY IS THAT MOST PEOPLE'S BRAINS JUST CAN'T DEAL WITH COMPLEX 3D SPATIAL DATA**

DANNY BROWN

And while it, along with the other pieces of software that aimed to do the same thing, were high on aesthetics, designers were never in too much of a hurry to start using it. It is suggested that the designers, who were already comfortable with Flash and Shockwave, were happier to struggle to create a 3D effect in these languages rather than to learn to use a new language altogether. Add to this that even broadband probably isn't fast enough to cope with this software and you can see the problems mounting already.

"As long as broadband is the fastest alternative, you will see that 3D Web environments will remain clunky," says Matt Owens. "Only if everyone could get connectivity that could stream content on the scale and calibre of a PlayStation 2 will you see 3D Web environments really take off."

But Danny Brown believes in something more fundamental than this. He says: "I think games and other entertainment sites will certainly adopt 3D technology. But the mainstream Web, no it won't. Fads for 3D navigation systems come and go, but the reality is that most people's brains just can't deal with complex 3D spatial data. It's often said that we live in a 3D world, and that seems to be the justification for these systems, but really humans live almost in a 2D world: we're very fixed to the ground, and that means we really only deal with spatial information in terms of navigation as 2D map information."

# THE TOOLS WILL KEEP EXPANDING TO SUIT DEVELOPERS' NEEDS AND NEW POSSIBILITIES

## DAMIAN STEPHENS

## 4.7 PLUG-INS – THE REST

There's a whole world of software tools for adding interesting new elements to your website. Many companies are trying to cash in on the success of Macromedia's Flash by creating the latest add-on for your browser. One relative success, for example, is the QuickTime Virtual Reality (QTVR) plug-in, which allows users to roam panoramic photographs, interact with photo-realistic animations, and play and listen to sound and video.

But the main problem is that users do not want to clog their system with more and more bits of software that they may use only once, that may conflict with other plug-ins and that use up valuable storage space. And designers are more than aware that, if a user visits a website and can't view it because they are lacking the appropriate plug-in, then they are more likely to simply go away than spend time and effort attempting to download and install the extra bit of software that they need.

This may seem like a negative statement to make, and might appear to hold no promises for the future of Web design, but all designers know that if something is demanded by them and the users, it will be developed and will be a success. Just as Flash came along at the right time, if you create the right piece of software at the right moment, the world may well be waiting to make you rich.

As Damian Stephens, creative director at the South African agency, No Organisation, comments: "The tools will keep expanding to suit developers' needs and new possibilities."

**IF A USER VISITS A WEBSITE AND CAN'T VIEW IT BECAUSE THEY ARE LACKING THE APPROPRIATE PLUG-IN, THEN THEY ARE MORE LIKELY TO SIMPLY GO AWAY THAN SPEND TIME AND EFFORT ATTEMPTING TO DOWNLOAD AND INSTALL THE EXTRA BIT OF SOFTWARE THAT THEY NEED**

## 4.8 WEB AUTHORING PACKAGES

To create a website, the very basics that you need are a text editor (Microsoft Word will do), an FTP (File Transfer Protocol) application for getting your Web pages on to your Web server, and a basic knowledge of HTML. But most people have access to much more than this.

The world's most popular piece of software for creating for the Web is Microsoft FrontPage. Most designers wouldn't agree that it's the best, but considering that it comes packaged with most new PCs that run Windows, you can't disagree with the statistics. The second most popular piece of software is called Dreamweaver, and the by now familiar company behind it is Macromedia.

Using both of these pieces of software couldn't be easier. If you've ever had to use a desktop publishing (DTP) package, then you will find yourself perfectly at home. Both allow you to visually place text and images, and both present it to you in a WYSIWYG (What You See Is What You Get) manner, so you know where your designs are going and how they are looking.

**ROLLOVER IMAGES THAT CHANGE WHEN THE MOUSE MOVES OVER THEM, MULTIPLE FRAMES, AND EVEN THE INCORPORATION OF FLASH ANIMATIONS ARE ALL EASILY MANAGED WITH DREAMWEAVER**

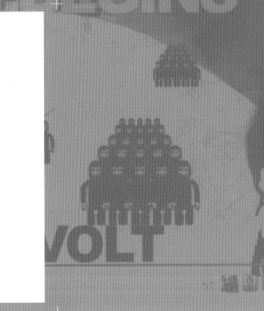

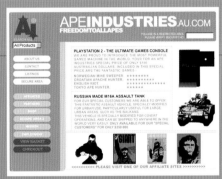

## //FLASH CAN BE USED TO TELL A STORY, PRESENT ARTWORK AND ENGAGE A USER

Simian is described by its creator, Ross Mawdsley, as experimental Flash narrative, and is a prime example of how Flash can be used to tell a story, present artwork and engage a user. In this particular case it does all three at the same time.

With Flash, Mawdsley has adapted themes from the Planet of the Apes film series into an ongoing series of projects that examine oppression, civil unrest, urban warfare and revolution. His work has received high-praise and has inspired many Flash programmers to take their own work in new directions. The design values alone, without the interactive elements, which make the ongoing story so gripping, are crisp and raw at once, and reflect perfectly the themes they are describing.

//AN ONGOING SERIES OF PROJECTS THAT EXAMINE
# OPPRESSION, CIVIL UNREST, URBAN WARFARE AND REVOLUTION

But Dreamweaver is a much more powerful package than FrontPage, and is favoured by many of the commercial Web design houses for website development, but is equally favoured by those who have little or no Web design experience. Its visual interface and functions allow the developer to program complex HTML without any specific knowledge of the code required. For example, rollover images that change when the mouse moves over them, multiple frames (more than one Web page on screen at once), and even the incorporation of Flash animations are all easily managed with Dreamweaver. But it is far more powerful than even this.

The tools and functions help to manage the workflow when building complex sites, allow designers to create dynamic pages which automatically update with new content and information, and help to create sites that are rich in information and experience. Once again, Macromedia has cornered the market of Web design.

Other packages, such as Macromedia Fireworks, BBEdit, Flash, Adobe Illustrator, Shockwave, Macromedia Director and even a standard text editor are all weapons to be found in the Web designer's armoury. What they use is particular to their style and way of working. What is certain is that there is no right way about it, and each designer will use what he or she requires in order to get the effect and the finished result they are looking for.

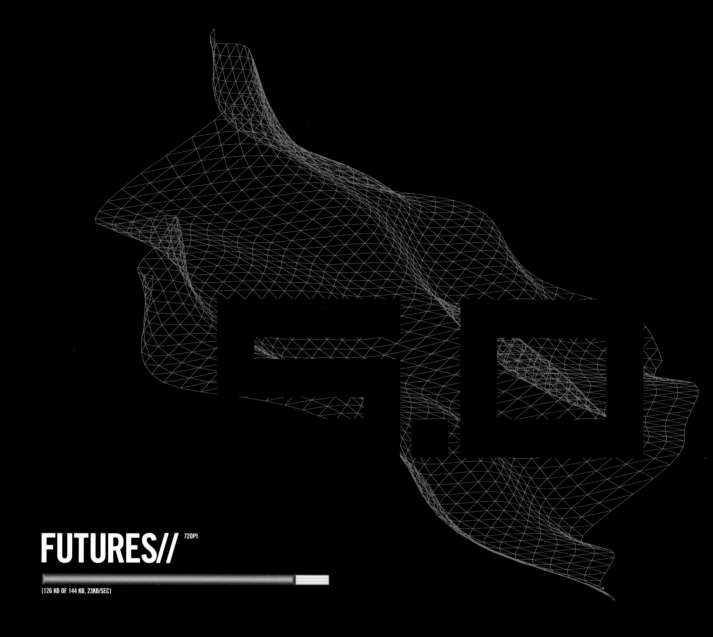

**FUTURES//** 72DPI

[126 KB OF 144 KB, 23KB/SEC]

# THE WEB HAS ALWAYS BEEN THE EMBODIMENT OF PROGRESS IN ACTION

For many who use the Web, the future is already here, and the designers who create for it are shaping the very world they inhabit. By pushing the technology to its limits, and always demanding more, they are the ones who are to thank for the constant development of new tools and technologies.

For many the Internet means the computer sat on their desk, but it is already becoming much more than this. Already, prototype homes have been created where everything from the curtains to the home entertainment system is wired to the World Wide Web. Toasters have been developed that check online weather forecasts and burn the appropriate symbol into your morning toast. There are cars on the road that can be examined remotely by engineers on the other side of the world, thanks to wireless Internet connections. There are even scientists, such as Professor Warwick from the UK's Reading University who are experimenting, much to the press' delight, with implanted chips, that allow sensors to monitor their location and even their nervous impulses.

And while much of this would have seemed like science fiction only a decade ago, no one can deny that this is the future, and it's happening now.

The same can be said for the creative Web. Designers who constantly push to make their sites do more in more ways, are shaping the future of our connected experiences, experiences that will be shared, and will often be unique.

**DESIGNERS WHO CONSTANTLY PUSH TO MAKE THEIR SITES DO MORE IN MORE WAYS, ARE SHAPING THE FUTURE OF OUR CONNECTED EXPERIENCES, EXPERIENCES' THAT WILL BE SHARED, AND WILL OFTEN' BE UNIQUE**

THE ONLY WAY TO
MOVE FORWARD
AND TO PUSH THE
ENVELOPE IS TO GO
BEYOND WHAT ANY
ONE SOFTWARE
PUBLISHER IS
ASKING YOU TO DO,
BY COLLECTING
YOUR OWN TOOLKIT
OF APPLICATIONS,
UTILITIES AND
TOOLS THAT ARE
PARTICULAR TO
YOU, YOUR AIMS
AND YOUR STYLES

JAMES THOMPSON

## 5.1 TOMORROW'S AUTHORING PACKAGES

The authoring packages of tomorrow will have to do much more than simply create websites, as the very definition of what a website is will be vastly different to that which we understand today. In the future creating an Internet site will be about creating for Interactive Television, for wireless hand-held devices, for wearable computer systems that are incorporated into our clothes and even devices that can project an image directly on to the retina of our eyes.

Already we are seeing designers using a whole arsenal of tools to create their sites, and it is highly unlikely that any one piece of software will meet the requirements of the future user. Indeed, it is highly unlikely that any one individual will be able to meet the requirements of the future user. Instead teams with a broad spectrum of knowledge and specialities will instead work together to create offerings spanning media, interface and platform.

As James Thompson, creative director at niche UK creative agency Wirescape.co.uk, explains: "You can't be limited by any single application, otherwise your work reflects these limitations. The only way to move forward and to push the envelope is to go beyond what any one software publisher is asking you to do, by collecting your own toolkit of applications, utilities and tools that are particular to you, your aims and your styles."

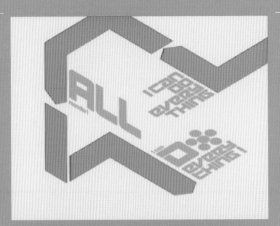

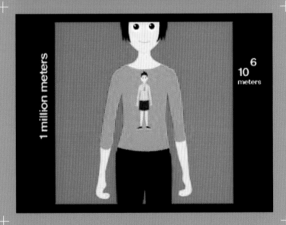

# GASBOOK
## CASE STUDY// DESIGN.AKIRA NATSUME // SOFTWARE.MIXED MEDIA

While most multimedia design relies heavily on the Internet, creatives are increasingly looking away from their screens for their inspiration and creation.

One such project is Gasbook by Japan-based Akira Natsume. It not only explores ideas such as visual design with its printed magazine, but also looks into ideas such as tactility, interaction, motion and even fashion. Each limited edition of Gasbook invites creatives to create projects in media such as ceramics, t-shirts and the now staple motion graphics and interaction of DVD and CD-ROM. Even the packaging of each issue is created by a participant, and in each different facet of the project there is always much to inspire and surprise. From music to animated shorts, coffee cups to clothes and video to print design, Gasbook is at the very cutting edge of publishing, and does for multimedia design, what Andy Warhol did for Campbell's Condensed Soup.

Generally each issue is based around a theme and in the past these have included "blue", "the cube", and "machine". Showcasing works by some of the most influential designers and groups, such as Tomato, Antirom, Hiroshi Saito and Katsumi Ishida, this publication explores every aspect of our lives as a forum for developing interactive design.

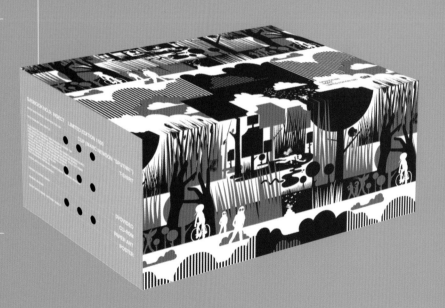

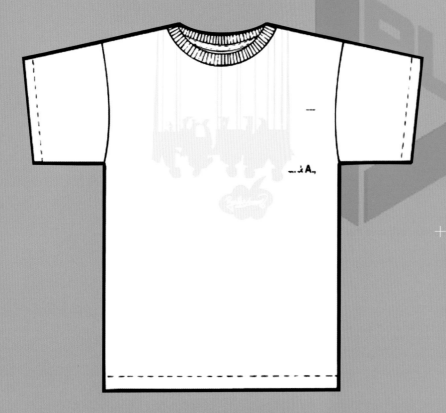

//THESE GIANTS CAME CRASHING DOWN, AND DOWN THEY CAME ONE AFTER ANOTHER, AND ALL WITHIN A MATTER OF YEARS

## 5.2 COMMERCIAL SEEPAGE

It has often been considered that commercial sites were the blander of the places to visit while wandering the Web. But increasingly this has started to change and one particular catalyst for the adoption by major corporate clients of a more creative approach to the Web, was the new economy bubble that burst towards the end of the 1990s.

Many of those Web design agencies that had grown to immense proportions by the rush of the corporate world to get online suddenly found that clients were unwilling to meet their huge fees, fees which were so high partly because the agencies were so huge. Few were surprised when these giants came crashing down, and down they came one after the other, all within a matter of years.

But a result of this was that corporations were turning to smaller design houses for their online requirements. Design houses where the focus was on the quality of work rather than the size of the bill, and where creativity had been the main motivator. As a result, major corporates started adopting more creative websites. They were taking bigger risks with regards the artistic values of their own sites. This seepage of the creative into the corporate started getting stronger and was seen in projects such as Sony's Connect Identity mixed-media offering, that embraced many different forms of media.

As a result, those larger agencies that did survive saw the benefit of spending more time on the artistic elements of a site, rather than simply churning out online brochure after online brochure. As a result, the more creative of those working in the medium are changing the way the world uses and exploits the Web. But according to Daniel Bonner, creative director at AKQA, one of the world's largest Web design agencies, this is nothing new.

He says: "History has a habit of repeating itself and you only have to take a look at the creative industries throughout the 20th century to see this transition occur time and time again. Take for instance the typographic 'art' and poetry of Stephane Mallarme that influenced the commercial poster in the early part of the century. The Web is no different to advertising or branding development in this respect. It is a creative communications vehicle which will go in search of diversity, a point of difference and an effective way to offer something new that will attract users to the experience."

The creatives behind the cutting edge of Web design are winning the battle for quality design online. Their work is finally beginning to be appreciated by the corporate masses, ever spurred on by the end user who demands more value, more quality – in a sense a return to a time when the customer was always right. How far this will go, however, is hard to ascertain.

Bonner explains: "Elements of interface design and digital experiments that are developed by a global community of designers, artists and technologists are sure to find their way into the commercial products that exist on the Web as the intuition, perceptions and behaviour of those using technology change. However the magnitude to which this will happen is difficult to forecast."

# HISTORY HAS A HABIT OF REPEATING ITSELF AND YOU ONLY HAVE TO TAKE A LOOK AT THE CREATIVE INDUSTRIES THROUGHOUT THE 20TH CENTURY TO SEE THIS TRANSITION OCCUR TIME AND TIME AGAIN

DANIEL BONNER

# SONY'S CONNECTED IDENTITY PROJECT

CASE STUDY// DESIGN.TOMATO INTERACTIVE // SOFTWARE.FLASH

Sony's Connected Identity project created by London's Tomato Interactive, is perhaps one of the most exciting, truly multimedia projects to have been embraced on the Web. Not only does it combine the corporate with the creative, but it also brings together TV, the Internet, input sensors, mobile phones and even stand-alone kiosks.

The idea behind the project was that members of the public in Japan could interact with the Web-based animations, changing them as they saw fit, and then their own influences would be incorporated into the end of each of Sony's television commercials.

Ant Rogers, from Tomato, explains: "The Connected Identity was born to bring the Sony brand into the hands of the people. It couldn't be more exciting. Any online

user can change the behaviour of Sony's image whenever they like. If at the same time you were playing around with their identity via the Internet and someone at a postproduction house needed to add the Sony end tag to their TV advert, your influence would be within that advert. This idea became a real-time living identity online. Now there exists a Shockwave viewer of the Connected Identity so users can see how it's changing in real-time. In Japan you can even load the Connected Identity on to your mobile phone. Sony's brand is always evolving."

The mesmerising scrolling images of dots actually contained hidden words that users could manipulate themselves, and if they were lucky their name and their word would make it on to television.

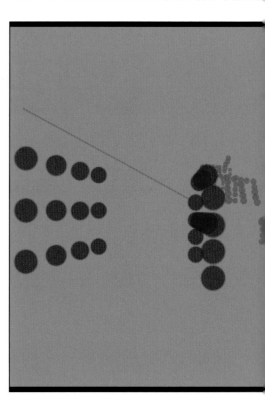

## connection is of

THIS IS THE SYMBOL DEMONSTRATING HOW SONY IS CHANGI

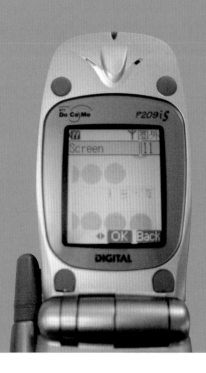

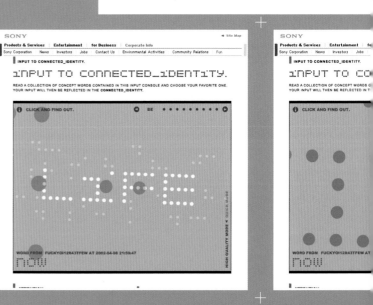

**ED.**

**IL TIME BASIS.**

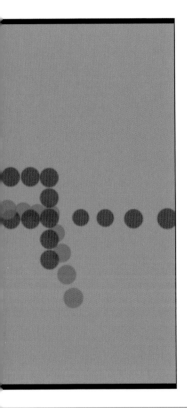

# connECTiOn iS OPEnED.

THIS IS THE SYMBOL DEMONSTRATING HOW SONY IS CHANGING ON A REAL TIME BASIS.

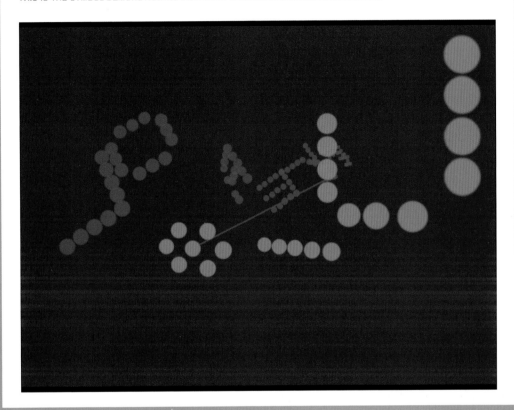

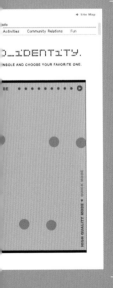

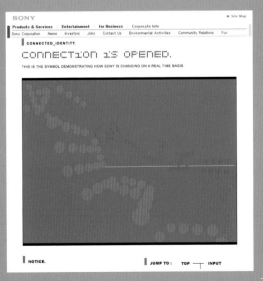

# //THE CONNECTED IDENTITY WAS BORN TO BRING THE SONY BRAND INTO THE HANDS OF THE PEOPLE. IT COULDN'T BE MORE EXCITING

**THE DEVELOPMENT OF THE INTERACTIVE EXPERIENCE ONLINE IS AND ALWAYS WILL BE CENTRED AROUND USERS. THE NEEDS, THE INSIGHTS, THE EXPERIENCES, THE BEHAVIOUR AND THE EXPECTATIONS OF THE USER ARE THERE TO BE PUSHED, STRETCHED, EXCEEDED, ADDRESSED, CHALLENGED AND THOUGHT ABOUT**

DANIEL BONNER

## 5.3 ATTACK ON THE SENSES, BEYOND THE CATHODE RAY TUBE

One thing that is certain is that the Web won't be attached to the computer display for much longer. We have already seen an enthusiasm for mixed-media works that combine kiosks, tactile devices, sound, vision, television, smell and even temperature to create new forms of output, and new forms of input.

In coffee shops in Scandinavia, thirsty visitors can avoid queuing by using their WAP cell phones to order their drinks in advance. Scientists have developed a fridge that keeps track of what food is inside, and when it begins to run out of certain products it automatically orders more.

But how much can we be sure that these are viable technologies for the future, rather than simply the big corporates chomping at the proverbial bit to be the first to get their hands on the next big thing. The Internet took the world by storm, as did SMS text messaging from mobile phones. Neither of these was intended to have the effect on the public that it did, but when commercial entities tried to repeat this phenomena with WAP phones, they failed miserably and all they could do was wave goodbye to the millions that had been spent on rushing the technology through. According to Daniel Bonner, they had overlooked one major thing. The users.

eat :: see :: listen :: think :: be

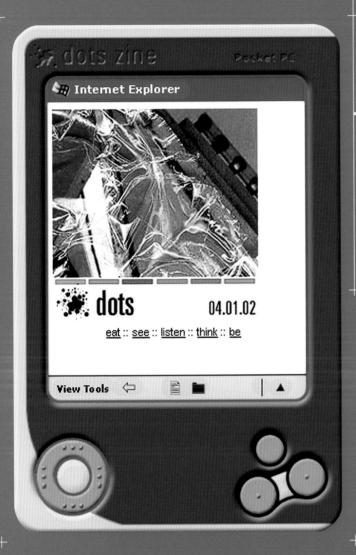

dots

04.01.02

eat :: see :: listen :: think :: be

# WWW.DOTSZINE.COM
## CASE STUDY// DESIGN.MOD7 // SOFTWARE.HTML

Designers are already starting to take advantage of futurist technologies, and before long, our future magazine reading may look a lot like Dots.

Dots, created by Canadian Web design company Mod7, is a design magazine created specifically for the small screen and smaller memory capacities of hand-held, mobile computers. Available at present for the Pocket PC and Palm Pilot, it previews art events, reviews restaurants and includes features of much interest to people who enjoy art and culture.

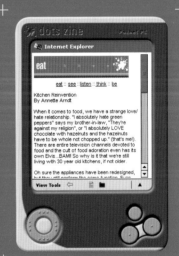

## //OUR FUTURE MAGAZINE READING MAY
## LOOK A LOT LIKE DOTS

Bonner explains: "If there is one group of people responsible for the way it has shaped itself I would have to say that it is the users. Whether it's the sheer frustration and despair that leaves you smashing both hands across your keyboard in the vain hope of eliciting a response on screen or the happiness that you get when that weekly shop turns up at your front door, on time. The development of the interactive experience online is and always will be centred around users. The needs, the insights, the experiences, the behaviour and the expectations of the user are there to be pushed, stretched, exceeded, addressed, challenged and thought about."

There is no way of telling where the future will take us, but it will be interesting to be a part of it, and perhaps even more interesting to see which of the next range of gadgets and gizmos will fall on the wayside. In 50 years' time we may well be rummaging through our attics when we come across a dusty Microsoft VR helmet in a box filled with Rubik's Cubes and Dealy Boppers. We'll laugh when we remember our Web connected Nike Air trainers, and we'll sit in amazement reminiscing about when we had to use our hands to type a document into Word.

But as James Thompson explains, it will be those companies that sit back and watch the users that will come through with the next line of killer apps, not those who jump the gun to pre-empt the next fad of consumerism.

He says: "It happens time and time again, but the companies never seem to learn. It happened with WAP, and it happened with the Sinclair C5. You can't assume you know what people want; you have to wait to be told. If that means putting your remotely accessed kettle on the back burner and potentially missing your big break, then so be it. But if you make a move and get it wrong, it can be your undoing."

**LaForet cube** (opposite)
This showpiece, developed by London's Tomato Interactive, shows how design technology and talent can be taken offline into the artistic world. Apparently suspended in space, this mysterious cube of blue liquid responds to the approaching footsteps of anyone close-by, by flickering and flashing in time to their pace.

ONE THING THAT
HISTORY HAS TAUGHT
US, HOWEVER, IS THAT
IT'S ALWAYS THE SMALL
GUY WHO COMES UP
WITH THE BIG IDEA.
FROM LITTLE ACORNS
COME MIGHTY OAKS

エレベーター
化粧室

## 5.4 A NEW ECONOMIC ORDER?

One thing that history has taught us, however, is that it's always the small guy who comes up with the big idea. From little acorns come mighty oaks, and looking at everyone who's made it big today, we can see that this is true. Even Bill Gates started off creating software to create school timetables, before going on to become the planet's richest man.

But today it's a very different world, and if the smaller, more creative companies are winning over the larger giants of commerce, then what can we expect to look forward to? Today, in this world of anti-capitalism, will we see smaller creative collectives shunning the power and responsibility that comes with greater commercial viability? Probably not, but we will see more acceptance of experimentation. The people creating for the Web today are doing it because they are fascinated by it. They are pushing forward ideas and projects that even the people who created the software they are using wouldn't have imagined. And they will keep doing it, as will the people who come after them.

But as the saying goes, power corrupts, and absolute power corrupts, absolutely.

## CREDITS

| | | |
|---|---|---|
| Andy Polaine | AntiRom | www.polaine.com |
| Damian Stephens | No Organisation | www.no-org.com |
| Sophie Rochester | Good Technology | www.goodtechnology.com |
| Andrew Milner | creator of Remote Access | www.chime.net.au |
| Ant Rogers | Tomato Interactive | www.tomato.co.uk |
| Victor Benady | Random Media | www.randommedia.co.uk |
| Cathy Olmedillas | Random Media | www.randommedia.co.uk |
| Andrew Johnstone | Design is Kinky | www.designiskinky.net |
| Danny Brown | Noodlebox | www.noodlebox.com |
| Vaughn Pratt | Stanford University | www.stanford.edu |
| Ajaz Ahmed | AKQA | www.akqa.com |
| Daniel Bonner | AKQA | www.akqa.com |
| Matt Owens | VolumeOne | www.volumeone.com |
| Hugh Mark | Axicom | www.axicom.com |
| Jakob Nielsen | Nielsen-Norman Group | www.useit.com |
| Harriet Gilbert | City University | www.city.ac.uk |
| James Thompson | Wirescape | www.wirescape.co.uk |
| JODI.org | JODI.org | www.jodi.org |
| Michael Schmidt | Kaliber 10000 | www.k10k.net |
| Julian Yap | ANSI/ASCII artist | www.geocities.com/SoHo/Gallery/4219 |
| Yohan Gringras | EvilPupil | www.evilpupil.com |
| Elizabeth Thornton | Tomato Interactive | www.tomato.co.uk |
| Mike Cina | WeWorkForThem | www.weworkforthem.com |
| Kenneth Aronson | Hell.com | www.hell.com |
| Daniel Achilles | Precinct | www.precinct.net |
| Jemma Gura | Prate | www.prate.com |
| Carlton Coulter | Aphexa | www.Aphexa.com |
| Ross Mawdsley | IKDA/Simian | www.ikda.co.uk |
| Francois Naude | alt.sense | www.altsense.com |
| Dominic Bolton | Dominic Bolton Photography | www.dominicbolton.com |
| Will Arndt | Mod7 Communications | www.mod7.com |
| David Womack | AIGA | www.aiga.org |
| Francis Lam | db-db | www.db-db.com |
| James Widegren | ThreeOh | www.threeoh.com |
| | etoy Corporation | www.etoy.com |
| Jeffrey Zeldman | | www.zeldman.com |
| Akira Natsume | Gasbook | |